GET THEM MOVING

HOW TO TEACH HISTORICAL MARTIAL ARTS

GUY WINDSOR

SPADA

Published in Helsinki, Finland, by Spada Press

ISBN 978-952-7157-08-4 (hardback)

ISBN 978-952-7157-10-7 (paperback)

ISBN 978-952-7157-15-2 (epub)

This one is for my daughters, Grace and Katriina. The best students and the best teachers I've ever had.

CONTENTS

PART I
INTRODUCTION

INTRODUCTION

Welcome to *Get Them Moving: How to Teach Historical Martial Arts*. My name is Guy Windsor. You probably knew that already, but a really useful first lesson for new teachers is to be very careful about assuming knowledge on the part of your students. And it's never wrong to go over the basics again.

This book is about you and your goals. What are you trying to teach, to whom, and why?

Before we get into that, you should probably know a bit about me, and what qualifies me to offer you advice on how to teach.

I have been teaching historical martial arts of one sort or another for well over twenty years, and it's my nature to refine anything I do regularly into a system. If I wasn't teaching swordsmanship I'd be teaching something else, because giving instruction is my best learning environment. If ever I'm having difficulty with any skill, be it woodwork, writing, or getting my sword to go where it should, I conjure up an imaginary student and in my mind teach them how to do it. Instant improvement, every time.

I began to study teaching with the same intensity that I bring to swordsmanship in 2010, which included attending a British Academy of Fencing coaching course. We trained from 9am to 9pm for five days straight, and I was deeply uncomfortable and out of my depth almost the entire time. Not very enjoyable, as such, but seriously good for me. It opened my eyes to a pedagogy of teaching, and crystallised for me a clear and simple set of goals for teaching. The Art of Arms is a way of organising the practices and principles of combat so that they may be studied and taught. The BAF has done to the art of teaching sport fencing what Fiore did for the art of arms. It is irrelevant that the techniques and theory of sport fencing are radically different to those of my core systems. What matters is that there is a clear body of technical and tactical knowledge, a perfectly defined environment in which it is supposed to be applied, and a systematic way to get students from one to the other. That system is priceless. Of course, what follows is not that system, it's my adaptation of their pedagogical approach to the goals of my Art and my School, but one should always acknowledge one's sources and influences.

You don't need to train in the same systems I teach to use this book. You can find all of the specific drills I use as examples here on our Syllabus Wiki, an online resource that my instructors use to help structure their classes. You can find the wiki here: https://swordschool.com/wiki/index.php/Main_Page

In my experience the single most common impediment to learning to teach is Imposter Syndrome, so we will deal with that first.

IMPOSTER SYNDROME

Let's start by defining our terms, so we can get a good look at the beast before we kill it. Then I'll go over several approaches for stepping up and teaching despite that horrid little whisper in the back of your head going "Why are you doing this? You're not good enough! Who the hell do you think you are?"

What is Imposter Syndrome?

The standard definition is:

> Impostor syndrome (also known as impostor phenomenon, fraud syndrome or the impostor experience) is a concept describing individuals who are marked by an inability to internalize their accomplishments and have a persistent fear of being exposed as a "fraud". The term was coined in 1978 by clinical psychologists Pauline R. Clance and Suzanne A. Imes. Despite external evidence of their competence, those exhibiting the syndrome remain convinced that they are frauds and do not deserve the success they

have achieved. Proof of success is dismissed as luck, timing, or as a result of deceiving others into thinking they are more intelligent and competent than they really are. While early research focused on the prevalence among high-achieving women, impostor syndrome has been found to affect both men and women, in roughly equal numbers. From Wikipedia: https://en.wikipedia.org/wiki/Impostor_syndrome

In short then, imposter syndrome is the cognitive fallacy in which people who are actually quite good at what they do nonetheless feel like a fraud doing it. They cannot say "I'm good at my job" or "I deserve to be taken seriously as an expert in my field."

People almost never have an accurate assessment of their own skill level. At the other extreme, the Dunning-Kruger effect is a cognitive bias which deludes incompetent people into thinking they are more competent than they really are. This is caused by their own inability to perceive their own incompetence; they are literally not fit to judge their own level. As I see it, we all live on the continuum between incompetent overconfidence, and competent uncertainty. A lack of confidence in your own infallibility is actually a mark of skill and experience, and it is normal for your ability to perceive your own level of skill to change relative to the skill itself. As you get better, your ability to see your mistakes gets better too, and so if all goes well there will never be a time when you think you're actually doing it perfectly. Get used to it!

Distinguishing between knowing your flaws and Imposter Syndrome

Let's be quite clear about the difference between imposter syndrome and feeling that you need to develop your skills. I'm a big fan of the Aristotelian model of virtue, where virtue is the midpoint between two vices. In other words any virtue taken to an extreme in either direction becomes a vice. If you are completely confident in your amazing expertise then you are as deluded as if you are completely confident of your amazing ineptitude. Virtue lies in between, where you can accurately assess your strengths and weaknesses, and work to strengthen your weaknesses and take advantage of your strengths, and thus get better at the thing you're trying to do.

Dealing with irrational fears

Imposter syndrome is an irrational fear. Despite external evidence of your competence, you have an irrational fear of being exposed as a fraud. Irrational fears are not easily dismissed by reason or evidence. If you are suffering from imposter syndrome then being suddenly presented with evidence of how competent you truly are isn't necessarily going to help. What may help would be reframing those feelings, and reframing the situation, to enable you to accomplish the thing that you are trying to accomplish, despite the imposter syndrome.

In my own experience of imposter syndrome, over a decade of gradually accumulating evidence that I was actually good at my job eventually did away with the idea that I wasn't a very good martial arts instructor. Getting a PhD for my research finally put paid to the feeling that I wasn't very good at the academic side. It would now feel false and weird to pretend I'm not an expert in my field. But oh lord it took a while. So the accumulation of evidence might help, but it might also just make you feel worse, because of another godawful cognitive bias, confirmation bias, which is your mind's tendency to notice and believe in evidence that confirms your existing opinions, and overlook or discount evidence that contradicts your opinions. So sufferers of imposter syndrome will remember every mistake, and forget the victories.

So who is this Windsor fellow to be telling me any damn thing?

My actual thought process was this:

"We need better instructors in the historical martial arts world, and I'm as experienced and well-qualified to teach this as anyone else. While no doubt there are many other instructors you could turn to, none have my own specific experience or approach, and so this may not be a complete waste of your time. And besides, many students have asked."

Though it may be true that there are others more qualified, I can still do this because:

a) I have a unique personal perspective,

b) I think if you want to become a better teacher you might be better off with this book than without it, and

c) My students asked for it.

These are the three main mental tricks I use to get round the problem, but each have their own strengths and weaknesses, so I'll unpack them.

What is my experience?

When I started my school in 2001 I was 27 years old, completely unqualified, and with very little experience. This was a classic recipe for imposter syndrome. Though I was unqualified to teach historical swordsmanship, there were no qualifications available, and the sense that I was not as good as my students deserved led me to study a lot, train a lot, and travel a lot to meet other instructors, and invite the best of them over to my school to teach seminars. It was a very sharp spur to growth.

Though feeling like a fraud was a good driver of improvement, it also led me into some awful mistakes. That's the real problem with imposter syndrome: it either stops you doing things altogether, which would be disastrous, or it drives you to make mistakes because you're coming from a position of inferiority. I was desperately looking for somebody to say "Yes, Guy, you have permission, here's a pat on the head." There was nobody out there who was qualified to say that, but I went looking for them anyway and sure enough, nature abhors a vacuum. I fell in with some people who gave exactly that kind of pat on the head but they were unfortunately not really qualified themselves in this field, and not only that, their whole approach was so different to mine that it was very counter-productive. Instead of growing and developing under their unqualified gaze I just felt even more inferior and useless and dreadful.

Keeping your students off-balance is a power play that some kinds of instructor use to keep students in their place. I was discussing this one night in a hotel room in Detroit with three of my instructor friends, and one of them looked at me and said "Guy, why do you give so much power to people who obviously don't like you very much?" That floored me. It was clear that I was giving my power away, and as the head of a school it was completely inappropriate, because giving away my power was giving my students' power away at the same time. Whatever power they had invested in me I was passing on without their permission to these people. This was bad in all sorts of ways.

Younger martial arts instructors often suffer from imposter syndrome, especially if they have not been properly trained to teach, and it is very often what leads them to being aggressive or bullying in class. They feel they have to be on top of the class and remain on top of the class to feel safe from being exposed as a fraud. And if anybody threatens their authority in any way then they have to beat them down quickly, because their entire sense of self is at stake. This explains much but excuses nothing.

Outside of the world of martial arts, you can see the same pattern, with imposter syndrome creating bullies, or preventing people from acting at all. I think we can agree then that imposter syndrome is a Bad Thing. So what do we do about it?

Will they be better off with this or without this?

This, to my mind, is the key solution. When producing anything (a book, a class, whatever), the question to answer is not "am I the best person to do this?", or "will this be perfect?"

The question is "will my readers/students/whoever be better off with this or without it?"

This comes up a lot for me when my students are readying themselves to start teaching. They know perfectly well that within my school there are many people who could teach that class better; people with a decade more experience, or even full-time professionals. Their gaze is in the wrong direction, looking ahead at their teachers, instead of back at their students. If the question is rephrased as "these students need a beginners' class tonight. Nobody else is available so it's either me taking it, or we cancel. Would they be better off with my class, or no class?" the problem disappears. This is why I get students teaching as early as possible, with the bar set at "can you maintain a safe environment?" not "can you transform these students into expert historical martial artists in record time?"

Using a gatekeeper

In some cases, it can be very useful to delegate the evaluation of your work to others. This is where your friends, martial arts teachers, or a professional editor can come in handy. My students start teaching before they feel ready, because practically nobody ever feels ready. But I train them for it, and they can safely leave it up to me to tell them when they're objectively good enough (I just encourage them at this point: I would never require them to teach a class). Mentors are good for this in every field. Friends are less good at gatekeeping, because they love you and think you're great. A bit like your mum. To be believable, they must be able to tell you your work is crap, so it's better to ask colleagues or acquaintances. Anyone you know well enough to ask, but who is not risking a long relationship if they don't like your work and your feelings get hurt. Which they will, because your work isn't perfect, and if they are any use, they'll show you the flaws, and that's painful but necessary.

Some further reframing ideas to get around the problem:

So what if you aren't that good?

When you drive a car you are responsible for a lot of lives: your own, your passengers', and every other road users'. And yet you do it. In martial arts, the worst case scenario is a student gets killed or badly injured. That's serious, and you must be competent to run a safe environment before you take a class unsupervised. But that's a rational fear, not imposter syndrome. Imposter syndrome will tell you that the worst case scenario is exposure as an incompetent. Put that in perspective with the consequences of running an unsafe class. Or indeed, driving badly.

The role of qualifications

Imagine you'd spent the best part of a decade in medical school, and are finally qualified as a doctor. To be sure, you'd be very aware of your lack of experience; you'd be a junior doctor. But a doctor nonetheless, and it would be absurd to pretend otherwise.

Qualifications that are attained through sustained effort and with an examining procedure that it is possible to fail can go a long way towards curing imposter syndrome, or at least providing a workaround.

Qualifications as a whole do three things:

1. They protect the patient. In fields where real harm can be done, rigorous training and examination are essential.

2. They protect the profit margins of the qualified. The higher the barriers to entry, the more you can charge. It's simple economics.

3. They give you permission. A pat on the head and a "you got this". This is especially true in areas where no qualification is strictly required to practise.

GIVE yourself permission to be good

It used to be that 'adult' was a noun, not a verb. But I've noticed that over the last decade or so people have been using it to describe behaving as an adult especially when they don't really feel like they're grown-ups: "I made a healthy breakfast and got the kids to school on time. Adulting achievement unlocked!"

This is imposter syndrome writ large: "I may be 40, employed, married, a parent, with a mortgage, etc etc, but I really feel like I'm about 12 and the whole big world out there is full of super-organised grown-ups and I'm not really one..."

But here's the thing: practically nobody feels like a proper grown-up.

Lois McMaster Bujold's book *A Civil Campaign* (1999) has a brilliant passage on this. One of the main characters, Ekaterin Vorsoisson, is speaking to a couple of younger women (the ellipses and italics are in the original):

> Adulthood isn't an award they'll give you for being a good child. You can waste… years trying to get someone to give that respect to you as though it were a sort of promotion or raise in pay. If only you do enough. If only you are good enough. No. You have to just… take it, give it to yourself, I suppose.

(From page 268 of the paperback edition, if you want to go read the whole conversation. Or even the whole novel, it's fantastic space opera.)

The difference between subject matter experts (or adults) with imposter syndrome and subject matter experts (or adults) without imposter syndrome is simply the ones without it have given themselves permission to be good at what they're doing. It is perhaps the most powerful thing you can do for yourself.

WHAT'S NEXT? Let's have a look at the different kinds of teachers we find in the historical martial arts world…

TYPES OF TEACHER

I've been knocking about the martial arts world for over thirty years now, and in that time I've studied under a lot of teachers. I've noticed that they tend to fit certain archetypes. Within each archetype you may find good or bad teachers, in that they are more or less able to impart knowledge and skills to their students, but some archetypes are obviously more problematic than others. Let's take a look:

Young black belt

"My art is the only art, and my teacher the only teacher". This is a common phase for students coming up through the ranks in a fairly traditional school environment. It can be prevented by the school being careful to expose the students to a wide range of other arts and instructors, and whoever is running the school to be seen to engage as equals with, not superior to, the visiting instructors. With luck, this phase passes quite quickly as the young black belt gets a broader experience. It's a problem because it makes the instructor blinkered in their approach, and makes them come across as arrogant.

If you find yourself thinking this way about your art, reframe it. "My art is the best art for me, and my teacher is the best teacher I know" is a totally different statement, because it leaves the mental doors open to a wider experience.

Gatekeeper

This type of instructor sees themselves as the guardian of the art they teach, and their primary duty to protect it from inferior students. Students will have to prove themselves worthy of being taught, usually by obedience to a shouty person. This of course implies that the art isn't robust enough to take care of itself! I was infected with a bit of this in the early stages of my career, but it was thankfully burned out of me by constant exposure to students who were clearly more worthy of the art than I was!

Warrior wannabe

There are a few martial arts that have been designed and developed for self defence in the modern world. They cover things like situational awareness, 'think like a criminal', operant conditioning, and one or two responses to common assault situations. But the vast majority of martial arts were designed and developed for entirely different scenarios. Kickboxing rings, for one example. The medieval duelling arena, for another.

If you expect your students to change out of street clothes for training, then you can be 99% sure you're not teaching self defence.

There are many instructors out there in love with the 'realness' of 'street fighting' (whatever the hell that is). You can tell them by the use of the term 'street effectiveness'. It is very unusual to find a person with actual combat experience (on the street or anywhere else) teaching like this. It's a problem because it's based on a romantic delusion, which you could infect your students with, and which could get them injured or killed through over-confidence.

Thankfully it's rare in historical martial arts. Literally nobody carries a sword for "street defence", so I would guess that you are not suffering from this. But you need to be aware of the syndrome when you interact with instructors from the wider martial arts world.

Parent

Once the testosterone and/or adrenaline has worn off a bit, an instructor will often become more parental in their approach. The student is a child to be brought up, in a kind and benevolent environment. This is clearly better than the young black belt, gatekeeper, or warrior wannabe, but is problematic in that unless they are running kids classes, it's infantilising. The overwhelming majority of the students I've had have been reasonable adults, and even those underage were capable of behaving like a reasonable adult. If you find yourself thinking parentally towards your students, hold on to the feeling of being responsible for their wellbeing while they train with you, but drop the associated feeling that they are in any way your children.

First among equals

In many HMA clubs, the instructor is explicitly just the 'first among equals'; the person tagged with running the class because they happen to have the most experience, or the most interest in teaching. Usually this encourages a more collegial learning environment, which can be a good or bad thing depending on the student's needs. Some students do learn better with a more formal instructor/student relationship. This can also engender a subtle form of gaslighting, in which the instructor appears to be first among equals, but the true dynamics are more authoritarian.

Professional instructor/ head of school

If you want to teach professionally, you will probably start by opening your own school. Making a living teaching historical martial arts is beyond the scope of this book. Assuming you are a good enough teacher that people will pay you for instruction, the trick is to get good enough at the business side of things that you can actually make a living. I am planning to write a follow-up book on making a living teaching historical martial arts, but in the meantime the best book on the subject that I've come across is *Starting and Running your own Martial Arts School,* by Karen Levitz Vactor and Susan Lynn Peterson.

Professional coach

This is a person hired by a club to teach them certain things, improve certain skills, but that's it. They are not formally part of the club at all, and have no administrative rank. It's a common model in, for example, University sports fencing clubs, but you can find it in many martial arts too.

For a long time, this was my core type, which developed into:

Consultant

My business card reads "Consulting Swordsman", because that's what I am. I'm not in charge of anyone— I'm a professional called in to solve problems or add new information. When teaching I'm responsible for the class's safety, so I'm required to set certain standards for behaviour (to wit: I expect everyone to behave like a reasonable adult, and everyone must finish class healthier than they started it). But I don't tell them what they should practice, or what their interests ought to be. They tell me what they want, and I do my best to deliver that. That could be 'please run a basic introduction to Fiore's longsword', to 'how do I keep my hands from getting hit in tournaments', to 'how do you do the punta falsa', or indeed anything else within my field. I only say no if I can't find a way to do it safely, or it's outside my competence, or it's outside the overall theme of the class as advertised. Though I have run a breakaway rapier class inside a supposedly medieval longsword seminar, because the students wanted it, and it could be safely done.

Historical Models, and our biggest challenge

We do have some examples from history of fencing masters and their students.

Fiore dei Liberi, who was never knighted, but taught knights, and possibly even the Marquis of Ferrara.

In the early 1600s Salvatore Fabris was fencing master to King Christian IV of Denmark. In 16th century London, Rocco Bonetti had a beautiful fencing school, with his noble students' coats of arms on the wall.

Domenico Angelo persuaded his aristocratic students to support the publication of his book in 1763— it's even dedicated to two princes (and in those days you couldn't dedicate a book like that without the person's permission).

The pattern is quite clear: the fencing master in European history has almost always been socially inferior to their clients. They had the same sort of relationship as a servant to a master, or a tradesman to a customer.

I mention this because by far the biggest impediment for most teachers is their giant ego. We want to be the centre of attention: "Welcome to the Guy Show!"

But a good teacher is focussed on their students, not themselves. It's not about us and what we want, it's about the students and what they need. This is perhaps the most difficult thing to learn, so it is the heart of this book.

So, what model does your teacher follow, what other instructor types have you come across, and what kind of teacher do you want to be?

In the next section we will look at the model I use for actually teaching...

QUESTIONS

Let's talk about you for a minute. What are your current circumstances, and what are your goals?

1. What kind of club and classes are you currently involved with?

2. What kind of classes do you *want* to run?

3. What are your ambitions as regards teaching historical martial arts?

4. What do you want to get out of this book?

5. Do you suffer from imposter syndrome, and if so how do you plan to deal with it?

6. What kind of teacher would you like to be?

7. What do you need to become that kind of teacher?

It's worth thinking about these questions, and perhaps writing down your answers, because they will affect how you should approach learning the craft of teaching.

PART II
OUR TEACHING MODEL

THE MODEL

Human beings are natural learning machines. It's our job as teachers to facilitate that, not interfere with it. The model I base all my teaching on is the way children learn to walk.

How do they manage it? Nobody explains the mechanics or neurology to them. They just see people do it, decide they want to do it too, and try. Every time they get it wrong, gravity provides the necessary feedback.

This is how we learn: we have a goal, we copy a model to reach that goal, and feedback mechanisms tell us how we are doing, so we adjust our actions.

A good goal is clearly articulated, and allows for definitive feedback.

A good model is clear and easy to copy.

A good feedback mechanism is immediate, specific, and unambiguous. When training a physical skill, the mechanism is ideally kinetic, not verbal or even visual.

. . .

Let's take learning to strike for example. What is the goal, what is the model, and what feedback mechanisms could we use?

Goal: hit the target

Model: strike with mandritto fendente

Feedback:

- Did I hit the target y/n?
- Hard enough y/n?
- Without shocking my joints y/n?
- From far enough away y/n?
- With the correct initiation y/n?
- With control y/n?
- If no target, you can use a mirror or a video camera to check form.

We normally choose one aspect of the blow to work on. Power or grip or footwork or timing or measure or edge alignment etc. For example, the buckler game is excellent for teaching timing, but useless for teaching power generation. If you don't know the drill, you can find it at guywindsor.net/bucklergame.

Notice how the feedback mechanism is immediate, kinetic, and clear. You either hit the buckler in time, or you don't. There is no need for any kind of clarification from the coach, and it is relatively easy to adjust the intensity to get the optimal rate of failure. Every drill has an optimal level of difficulty: if it's too easy, the student won't learn, and if it's too hard, they'll get frustrated. We measure the difficulty by how often the student 'fails'— misses the target, gets hit, or whatever. For most students and most drills, the optimal rate of failure is between 20 and 40%. In short— if they are successful 3 or 4 times out of 5, they're probably learning. 5 out of 5, it's too easy; 2 out of 5, it's too hard. The purpose of the feedback mechanism is to let the student identify success and failure.

. . .

EVERY DRILL, technique or action should be a solution to a problem that the student has experienced. When you want to teach a technique or concept, you should generate the problem first. This allows the students to internally generate the goal of learning that particular thing, rather than you imposing it from outside.

When beginners show up to your beginners' course, it is because they have identified a problem (such as "I like swords but don't know how to use them"), and are expecting a solution to that problem (though they don't usually see it that way themselves).

Teach a parry/riposte as a solution to a previously experienced strike. Teach the counter to the parry as a solution to getting parried.

This is true at every level. For instance, at a class I taught recently I identified lack of fencing memory as a problem in my students. Rather than just teach them our fencing memory drill (see 06.01 Preparing for Freeplay if you don't know it), I set them a task that required a decent fencing memory: they had to fence to one hit, then reproduce the hit, and let the one who got hit work on preventing or countering it.

Sure enough, after a little while of doing that obviously useful exercise, I asked them if they could reliably reproduce what just happened... or whether we should spend some time on developing their fencing memory.

They would have trusted me to just teach them the fencing memory drill and believe it to be useful, but having them experience the problem first made it much easier for them to learn the solution.

CHANGE THE ENVIRONMENT, not the student

The combination of the model and the feedback mechanism creates a natural learning cycle in which the student cannot help but improve towards their goal. Adjust the training environment such that the desired behaviour is rewarded. If you want your student to make a longer strike, move the target further away and they will naturally reach for it. If you want them to riposte faster, leave a smaller window for them to riposte into, and they will naturally speed up to hit you in time.

If you find yourself making technical corrections (bend your knees! Put your weight on your back foot!) then the student will learn these corrections very slowly, because they have to remember them. But if you make it so that the thing they are trying to do only works if they bend their knees, or have their weight on the back foot, or whatever else, then they will learn it very quickly. All they have to do to retain the correction is keep doing the thing in a way that actually works.

This is a very simple idea, but can be very hard to do in practice. Simple does not mean easy.

If you can't generate an environmental pressure that creates the desired change, you should ask yourself why you want the student to make that correction. What is it giving them? What does it actually do? If you don't know the answer to those questions, then why are you demanding this change?

Ideally you will always create a learning environment in which the student naturally improves without intervention. When you are helping your students master a particular skill, the question you should be asking yourself is 'how should I change the environment so the student's action will naturally change in the desired way?'

This is the very essence of my teaching approach, and the thing I am trying to teach you. As you might expect by now, it absolutely requires you to be focussed on your students and what they are doing, not on yourself and what you want to teach.

Teaching is, and often should be, a stealth activity. Let me take a charming example: my kids learning to cook.

Cooking is one of the most important skills a human being should have. If you can cook, you can exert some control over your diet. Your diet represents probably 30% of your long-term physical health (with exercise and sleep being the other 70%). If you can't cook, you are at the mercy of family, friends, restaurants and corporations for what you can eat. The first two in that list probably have your best interests at heart. The other two? Not so much. So it's essential parenting to make sure your kids can cook.

The key ingredients in cookery are:

1) Recipes. You can use other people's or invent your own, but you do need some kind of blueprint.

2) Ingredients. You must be able to find and select the ingredients that are right for your recipe.

3) Cooking techniques: chopping, boiling, frying, baking etc.

To this end, we let our kids watch shows like Great British Bake Off, YouTube channels like Tania Burr, Nerdy Nummies and so on, because children copy what they see, and while this does tend to encourage some odd habits and turns of phrase (some baking is always done in an American accent in our house), it also leads to exchanges like this:

"Daddy, I want to make a [insert name of vile sugary thing here]"

"Ok, make a shopping list".

The child then gets a piece of paper, and writes out the ingredients (see how we sneak in some writing practice there?), and we go to the shops. In the shop, we find the ingredients. The kids have to read the labels, and make sure they have enough of everything (for which they need arithmetic). We then buy it, go home, and get to work. Of course, boring old daddy doesn't like watching the video in the kitchen; oh no, the instructions need writing out too! ("I don't want flour on my mobile phone…")

And then we follow the instructions, make the triple-caramel-quad-choc-sprinkle-covered diabetic extravaganza, and eat it, to all-round delight.

The point is, by letting them follow their own interests, we create a momentum in the direction of 'command of diet'. Now all we have to do is to gently steer that momentum in a healthier direction: "we can only eat that after dinner. So what shall we have for dinner?"; "kids who come shopping get to choose what we eat"; that sort of thing.

All of this is why my elder daughter can bake pizza from scratch, makes a mean chicken pie, and has very strong opinions about "store-bought" pastry. My younger daughter is less interested, and so less skilled, but it's still perfectly normal for her to choose something she wants to make, and set about establishing the recipe, choosing the ingredients, and making it, commandeering whatever help she needs in the process.

The major downside is we eat far more crap than we otherwise would: it plays hell with my low-fast-carb diet. But it's worth it in the long run because whatever diet my kids choose to follow as adults, they will be able to make from scratch, and control exactly what goes into it. I hope they'll choose wisely, but whether they do or not, at least they will have the choice.

I take the same attitude towards teaching swordsmanship. It's not for me to sneer at a student who secretly wants to be an elf, or even an Ewok. Whatever brings them to the sword is inherently good. It's then up to me to gently steer that momentum in a more rewarding direction. This is why I begin all my classes by asking the students what they want. Sure, sometimes they ask for things that are bad for them, so I redirect things a little but make it clear that it's the closest I can get them to the goal they set. It would be fundamentally counter-productive to shut them down or bring their enthusiasm to a sudden stop.

This reminds me of steering a boat. When the boat is stationary (also known as 'dead in the water'), you can't steer it at all; but when it is under way it takes only the gentlest touch to guide it right or left. Sometimes, a wave might hit and bash the ship off-course. Then you let it go, and when the crisis passes a moment later, another gentle touch brings it back to the mark.

That's how it should feel when you're teaching.

Next up, let's take a look at the environment...

CREATING THE ENVIRONMENT

By far the most important thing you do as a martial arts instructor is create a safe training environment. Martial arts are physically and psychologically dangerous, and it's up to you to keep your students safe within reason.

Here is how you do that.

1. The Culture

By far the most important safety feature of any club or school is its culture. Incoming students will generally adapt to whatever culture they find, or quit. So it's your job to make sure that the school's culture is one of safety and mutual respect. If unsafe behaviour is always frowned upon and has negative social consequences, people won't do it.

You create this culture by modelling the behaviour you want, encouraging students to copy it, and by stepping in and interrupting any unsafe behaviour you see. If you want students to always wear a fencing mask when they drill, then always wear a fencing mask when you drill, and don't let anyone drill without one.

2. The Physical Space

Ideally, you will have access to a physical space that is clearly defined, and to which you have exclusive access during training. In other words, random people can't show up, grab a sword off the wall or out of a bag left open on the floor, and start arsing around. A dedicated salle space is nice to have, but most clubs train in rented school gyms, church halls, or outside. It is much easier, especially for a less experienced instructor, to control an indoor space. There are fewer variables to take into account. But if you are training outside, it's worth roping off the space you'll be using, to create a psychological barrier between your training area and the rest of the world. This helps the students stay in the zone (physically and mentally), and helps keep the curious out of the way of moving swords.

Whatever the space, you should check the floor for debris, broken glass, etc. especially if you may be practising throws. It is good psychological practice to prepare the space before class by cleaning it in some way— mop the floor if you're indoors, or pick up litter if you're outside. This makes it safer, but most importantly establishes your psychological ownership over the space.

3. The Psychological Space

Successful training requires students to practice at the optimal rate of failure. This means that they will all be failing a lot. This can be a real problem for students who are not used to the idea of failing in public being okay. As the teacher it's your job to be seen to fail usefully, and to normalise failing at the optimal rate by modelling it for the students. The environment you create should be supportive and kind, but also disciplined and honest.

4. Equipment

Your equipment cannot keep you safe. People get killed in full plate armour, in tanks, in bunkers. There is no level of physical protection that will prevent injury if your training practices are unsafe. The problem with safety gear is that it fosters the illusion of safety. I shatter the illusion by showing students a fencing mask that we attacked with daggers, swords, and a pollaxe. It failed catastrophically.

You wear safety gear to *allow your training partners to actually make contact*. This *increases* the risks.

But if used correctly, safety equipment allows you to train in ways that would be unsafe without it. Wearing steel gauntlets, you can practice striking at the hands (but not very hard). Wearing masks, you can thrust to the face (but not very hard). Wearing full freeplay gear and using training swords adapted for fencing (sufficient flex, rubber tips etc.) allows you to fence each other, and provided you control the level of force, nobody gets hurt.

It's the culture of safe training that keeps people safe, not the equipment.

5. Feedback

Every environment provides certain kinds of feedback. As the instructor, it's your job to make sure that the feedback the students are getting leads to the desired behaviour. This is as true when it comes to creating safe fencing culture as it is when rewarding an accurate riposte and punishing a sloppy one. People learn naturally from interacting with their environment. So, to change behaviour, change the environment.

. . .

NEXT UP ARE five guidelines for how to use language when teaching...

LANGUAGE AND HOW TO USE IT

How you use language will have a huge impact on your students. Martial arts are primarily about physical skill, so when teaching you will need to adjust your language such that it helps, not hinders.

Here are the five basic ideas around language that I use:

1. **Speak less, do more**. Unless you are giving a lecture on a theoretical topic, give just enough information that the students know what to do next, and get them moving. One of the best classes I ever taught was with a raging case of laryngitis. I couldn't speak at all, so I had a small whiteboard, with four words on it: Beginners, Intermediates, Structure, and Flow. I'd clap to get their attention, show them something, and indicate which group should focus on what. Zero chat. Everyone loved it.

2. **Use only positive constructions.** The subconscious mind does not process the negative parts of a statement. "Do not think of a pink elephant" will have just about everyone visualising a pink elephant. "Keep moving" is better than "don't stop". "Relax" is better than "don't be stiff".

3. **Use external frames of reference**. Wherever possible, refer

to things outside the student's body. Even really subtle differences like "point your shoe towards your opponent" works better than "point your foot towards your opponent". Rather than have students move "straight ahead", have them move towards a specific point that is straight ahead of them. "Reach for the sky" is better than "put your hands above your head".

4. **Name the feeling.** When your student is moving the way you want them to, it should feel powerful, smooth, fast, easy, or something similar. This way of moving is composed of millions of tiny decisions their brain is making to create the motion, which are very hard to separate out, so don't try. Just have them give a name (in the language of their choice) to the feeling of moving like a martial artist, and share it with you. That way when they start to move clunkily, you can just murmur that one word, and that will remind them of how the movement *should* feel. Incidentally I'm the only instructor I know who does this, but I hope it catches on because it works really well.

5. **Avoid technical corrections.** Where possible, you should adjust the external environment to generate the change you want. Let's say you have a student that is cutting short. Get them to make longer blows by moving the target further away. If you put the command "reach further forwards", or "extend your arms more" into their head, that command will persist long after the need for it has passed, and they will almost certainly learn to over-extend. So get the cut to the right length, and then have them name the feeling.

IT'S ALMOST a certainty that you will violate all of these guidelines, in every class. Almost every instructor I've ever trained with has talked too much, used negative statements, used internal frames of reference, named the thing not the feeling, and pestered me with technical corrections. And I do all those things too. It's natural.

And sometimes necessary: if a drill won't go right until the beginner has her left foot forwards, and she just can't see which way round your feet are when you show her, just say "left foot forwards".

But when in doubt, speak less, use positive statements and external frames of reference, name the feeling, and avoid technical corrections.

Alternatives to language

So if we're not supposed to talk much, how do we communicate? Actions speak louder than words: demonstrate what you want the students to do. This is true for every aspect of your school's culture not just teaching class.

Talking about how you wish more women would stick around and become senior students is much less powerful than choosing women students to demonstrate with.

Telling students they should do their strength training and remedial work (like massage) is good: but spending time before or after every class doing your own remedial work is a much stronger message.

When in class, you will obviously demonstrate what you want the students to do. But what if you have a student who has a habit of (for instance) dropping their back arm? You could bring it to their attention by telling them, but it's more effective to tap them lightly on the arm. I use a stick for this, as it's less personal than using my hand. I do mean lightly— this is not punishment, it's just a gentle tap to bring their mind into the body part that you want them to pay attention to. Though of course that's an internal frame of reference, so it would be better to adjust the environment such that keeping their arm where it should be is natural.

. . .

You teach that which you most need to learn

I'm a writer. My undergraduate degree was in English Literature. I'm all about precise use of language, but most of all, about *abundant* use of language. I can walk into a lecture hall full of people, with zero preparation, and talk for two hours. I've done it more than once.

One of the many reasons I love swordsmanship is because you can't argue your way out of a cut to the head. It's fundamentally not a linguistic phenomenon, so it forms a beautiful counterbalance to the otherwise incessant chatter in my head.

So I've had to learn all five of my guideline ideas the hard way. The trick for me was to be pretty ruthless about what was working for my students, and ignore what felt really natural to me.

You may have noticed that this book is entirely language. This is because I am trying to communicate a theoretical structure for you. There is literally no way for me to teach you how to teach without talking, unless I just made you watch videos of my classes until you absorbed how I do it. This way is more efficient.

So language has its place, but in martial arts instruction, its place is sitting quietly in the corner.

PART III
TEACHING CLASSES

FUNDAMENTALS OF TEACHING A BASIC CLASS

Teaching a basic class can be quite daunting for an inexperienced instructor. The purpose of this section is to give you a set of guidelines for organising and teaching a basic class.

There are, generally speaking, three kinds of class: beginners' course, basic class, and advanced class. Of these, the basic class is perhaps the easiest. Beginners are hard to teach well because they have absolutely no frame of reference; you have to build that for them. They have to be taught everything, from how to safely take a sword off the rack, to how to do a push-up. In a basic class, everyone has at least the beginnings of a common frame of reference. They know at least the choreography of some drills, and have understood the group's safety protocols. At the advanced level it can appear very challenging to teach well, because you have to be able to move people along who are already quite skilled. But as you will see when we get to it, it's actually not that hard.

HIERARCHY OF GOALS

At the basic level, you have a simple hierarchy of goals:

1. Safety
2. Teach one thing
3. Inspire them
4. Get out of the way.

1. Safety

Your job as the instructor is really simple. At the basic level, it is to provide a safe environment in which training will occur. That's it. You don't need to be able to teach the *punta falsa* from first principles, nor customise the class to the interests of its members: just open the doors, give folk stuff to do, and make sure no-one gets hurt. In short: create and maintain a safe training environment. Get everyone to the end of class without injury. The prime directive is this: "everyone finishes class healthier than they started it". Swordsmanship is naturally dangerous, so this overrules all other goals. An airline pilot thinks the same way. It's vastly more important that everyone survives the flight than that they get to the destination airport at the scheduled time. You do this by making sure that all students present are aware of the dangers, and have a set of safe practices to follow.

2. Teach one thing

So long as it doesn't conflict with the prime directive, your next goal is to teach them one thing. That could be a technique or drill they didn't know before, or how to apply a drill they already know. One thing per class. Not more! The most common mistake a junior instructor makes is to try to pack it all in. That one thing might be "control of measure", for instance; in which case you use only drills they already know to apply that skill; or the one thing might be teaching the steps of a new drill, in which case you go easy on the measure. You might sometimes get in two, or even three things into a basic class, but less is usually better.

When teaching, always, always, start with something they can already do, then modify it towards what you want them to do. For example, assuming an able-bodied class (but the rule holds even more strongly for disabled students), if you want them to learn a particular passing step, start with simple walking. Everyone can do that. Great. Then do the step again, but modify it towards the specific kind of stepping your style demands. An upright body, for instance: do the step again, with an imaginary bowl of single malt whisky on your head. Don't spill a drop! In this way, everything you teach them is a modification of something they can already do. This makes it much less confusing, and gives them a stable base to work from. When I teach beginners to cut with a longsword, the process goes like this:

1. Swing the sword from shoulder to shoulder, standing still. Stay relaxed.

2. Swing the sword from shoulder to shoulder, aiming at head height (most students do the previous step aiming at the floor, like golfers).

3. Swing the sword and follow it with a step each time. Make sure the correct foot is stepping.

4. Swing the sword with the step, and adjust the line to the one Fiore shows (jaw to knee).

5. Swing the sword along the line with the step, and align the edge with the blow.

6. Swing the sword along the line with the step and with the edge aligned, pausing at the moment of maximum extension.

7. Swing the sword along the line with the step and with the edge aligned, gently tapping your partner on their mask.

Everybody can do step one. And very soon, usually under 20

minutes, everyone can do step seven safely and with acceptable technical accuracy.

You might ask, what is the "one thing" I'm trying to teach you right now? Fundamentally, I want this book to give you the confidence to stand up in front of a class and do your best. That's it. Please do let me know if it's worked!

3. Inspire them.

So long as it doesn't interfere with the "one thing", or the prime directive, your next goal is to inspire the students with the sense that they can do this. They can become the martial artist they want to be. It is usually not helpful to dazzle them with your skill; it is much more useful to surprise them with how much they can do, with a little help. A little flash and dash goes a long way, but as a general rule, only show them the things you want them to actually do. It should be just outside their current competence, but they should be able to touch it. One thing I cannot stand is attending a seminar in which the instructor puts on a show, however glittering; it should never be about what the teacher can do; only about what the students can do.

The most inspiring message you can give them is "you can do this". Swords are cool. Swords are aspirational. Your students probably aspire to be excellent fencers. Show them the path that will take them there.

4. Get out of their way.

So long as it conflicts with none of the above, your job is to create an environment in which learning happens naturally. Then get out of their way, do not interfere, and let them practise. This, for most instructors, is the hardest step. You can see the errors they are making, and you want to dive in and fix them. So, the question is, when should you? I use a rule of three: see the mistake once, ignore it. See it twice, watch to see if it happens again. On the third time, make the one most basic correction. To identify that one correction, you need a hierarchy of correction.

Every time anybody does a drill or technique, no matter the level (and I include the best martial artist you have ever seen or heard of in this), there is always something to improve. As an instructor your job is to identify one thing they should change, and bring it gently to their attention. Usually, especially in a basic class, there are lots and lots of visible errors. So the question is, which one first?

1. Start with gross choreography. If the drill needs to be done with the left foot forwards, or the feed is a cut to the head, but the student is starting right foot forwards, or thrusting to the belly, fix that. No technical correction (such as how they should do it).

2. If there are no gross choreographical errors, then identify the technical error that is interfering most. Measure is the most common. Failing to organise the body properly behind the action (aka grounding or structure) is also very common.

3. If the measure is ok, and the timing ok, then finally go to the internal specifics, such as their groundpath, or the slight unnecessary tension in their shoulder.

Making corrections

The goal of any correction given while the student is practising is always to improve the student's immediate performance of the drill in question. This is not the time for lengthy explanations, or teaching them something new. This is so very context-dependent that I think it's impossible to give you a comprehensive list of how and what to do, so here are some simple guidelines that will help in 99% of situations.

• Correct one thing at a time. At any given moment, the student should be focussed on only one thing. Let everything else slide while they get that one thing under control.

• Correct the biggest, most obvious mistake. Leave the rest. Generally, correct by telling them what to watch while you show them the action again. Such as "watch my feet", or "watch how the sword moves". Having paid attention to the way you're doing the thing they were doing wrong, they will usually make the necessary change without really thinking about how they were doing it before.

• Use only positive statements. "Do not keep your left leg straight" is not very helpful. "Bend your left knee" is better. But best of all is to set up an exercise in which the student naturally bends their leg the way you want them too, without thinking about it, because it helps them accomplish a goal they understand. For the knees, I usually use grounding and mechanics exercises to give the student the experience of doing the exercise with the leg bent and it working better, feeling better, so they will naturally keep doing it.

• Show them how you want it done, a couple of times. Let them try. Show them again if needed.

• Keep verbal technical correction to an absolute minimum. It's better to tap the offending leg to remind them than to say "bend your knee", because the language centres in the brain are not involved with making physical movements other than speech.

• Praise effort, acknowledge success.

NEXT UP, let's look at how to structure a basic class...

STRUCTURING AND PLANNING A BASIC CLASS

It is very useful to establish a basic structure for your classes. It allows you to progress naturally from the simple to the complex, and it establishes a set pattern within which you can add variation without losing your way. It's good for the teacher because it creates a framework with which to construct your class plan, and it's good for the students because it makes one aspect of every class predictable, which reduces confusion.

The structure of a typical basic class in my school looks like this:

1. Opening salute
2. Warm-up
3. Footwork/mechanics specific to the system
4. In Armizare (Fiore) classes, we usually have a long section on dagger or wrestling related to the sword material we'll be doing
5. Solo sword practice
6. Pair sword practice, working from simple towards complex
7. End salute.

Within each section there should be a typical structure: for example, the warm-up usually goes something like:

1. Open joints
2. Heat body
3. Activate stabilisers
4. Establish range of motion specific to the style
5. Establish smooth movement

The content of each section is determined by the theme of the class (see below, "How to Write a Class Plan" for more on theme). For beginners, it may be just teaching them some specific footwork actions, but more usually, it's about preparing the students to do the sword material better. The solo sword practice likewise; I focus on the mechanics that the students will need for the pair drills, unless mechanics are the theme. It's a good idea to structure each section with a progression from basic towards more advanced or complex actions, so as the class progresses from section to section, the material is going from simple to complex to simple again, in the form of a wave.

There is no way to predict exactly who will show up to a given class, or what their interests will be, so in general I don't plan my classes at all in advance; we do it in the first few minutes of the class itself. But I've been doing this a long time, so I don't need time to think about how to put the pieces together. For less experienced instructors I highly recommend that you plan your classes beforehand, at least in broad strokes. It's also a good idea to then let everyone know what the subject will be, so they know what to expect.

How to Write a Class Plan

Start by deciding your theme: what exactly do you want the students to know or be able to do by the end of it? If possible, ask the students what they would like to cover, giving yourself time to plan the class before it starts. "Controlling measure", for instance. Or "survey the content of level 2 in our curriculum". Or "using counterattacks". Or "sword handling". Then block out the allotted time, in 10 minute chunks. So a ninety minute class has nine chunks. The warm-up is usually the first one or two chunks (two if you are teaching the exercises from scratch; one if you are just running through them for students who have done them before). A good class has a clear connection between each of its parts; a story that the students can follow, with every drill related to the one before it and after it, and the theme running as a clear guideline throughout.

It is really helpful to distinguish between breadth and depth. A class will usually focus on broadening the student's knowledge base, or adding depth to their skills. You must begin with breadth; beginners do not know very much to start with, so teach them something new. But once they know a few things, start helping them to get better at the things they already know, rather than keep adding new material. The trick is that adding breadth is easy, especially for an inexperienced teacher. "Here is this cool new technique". It's an easy win. But it is essential that you are also able to add depth. "So you know this technique. Ok, now let's apply it in more and more difficult circumstances." You do this by applying one or other of your multipliers: who moves first, add a step, degrees of freedom, and the Rule of Cs.

If you're not familiar with the multipliers, you'll find them in the Skill Development chapter (starting on page 95), but in short, once they have the basic choreography, one student in each pair should be coaching the other in a specific skill.

Let me run you through a sample rapier class plan, for a class starting at 6pm. You can find each of the drills I mention on video on our online Syllabus wiki, here: https://swordschool.com/wiki/index.php/Main_Page

Time	Content: Teaching the Attack by Cavazione to students who don't know it well.
Before class	Planning. Establish theme: attack by cavazione. Select and order exercises and drills.
18.00	Salute. Everybody must know that class has started.
18.01-18.10	Warm up. Theme requires lots of lunges, so emphasise the necessary flexibility and stability for them.
18.10-18.20	Footwork exercises, related to the theme, so emphasis on the lunge. We use the "Rapier Footwork form" as our starting point, usually.
18.20-18.30	Mechanics exercises, related to the theme. "Hunt the debole."
18.30-40	Teach the basic action as a technical drill.
18.40-18.50	Plate 7, emphasis on step two, the attack by cavazione. The counter shown on plate 7 (step 3 of the drill) is done by the coach in the drill, to improve the attack, not defeat it.
18.50-19.00	Plate 16, same emphasis.
19.10-19.20	Plate 15: contracavazione: using an attack by cavazione as a defence against itself.
19.20-19.30	Review the basics again. Allow free choice of which exercises to repeat.
19.30	End salute. Every class must have a clear end-point.

. . .

FOR STUDENTS who already know the material, it's time to focus on training them to use it. A class on the same topic to a more advanced group might look like this:

Time	Content: Training the Attack by Cavazione for students who already know it well.
Before class	Planning. Establish theme: attack by cavazione. Select and order exercises and drills.
18.00	Salute.
18.01-18.10	Warm up. Theme requires lots of lunges, so emphasise the necessary flexibility and stability for them.
18.10-18.20	Footwork exercises, related to the theme, so emphasis on the lunge. We use the "Rapier Footwork form" as our starting point, usually.
18.20-18.30	Mechanics exercises, related to the theme. "Hunt the debole."
18.30-40	Review the basic action briefly, then straight into Plate 7, emphasis on step two, the attack by cavazione. The counter shown on plate 7 (step 3 of the drill) is done by the coach in the drill, to improve the attack, not defeat it.
18.40-18.50	Plate 16, same emphasis.
18.50-19.00	Tactical drill: attack by cavazione if you think it will strike; otherwise step away instead. Use "hunt the debole, with footwork" as the base for this.
19.10-19.20	Tactical drill: draw the attack by cavazione onto your prepared defence (eg Plate 7, 16, or allow free choice of plates the students know).
19.20-19.30	Review the material briefly. Allow free choice of which exercises to repeat.
19.30	End salute

As you can see, the material gets more and more tactical, and with a significant degree of freedom allowed so that students can progress at their own pace.

To help you plan your classes you will find class planning handouts at guywindsor.net/classplans.

Next up, let's look at actually teaching and running the class...

TEACHING AND RUNNING A BASIC CLASS

Demonstrate, Explain, Demonstrate, Practice

Your class plan is broken up into ten minute blocks. Within each of these (apart from the warm-up), you will usually need to show the students what to do, then let them practise. Every keen young instructor I have ever seen shares a common failing: we all talk too much. What should be a one-minute demonstration becomes a fifteen-minute lecture. When teaching teachers, I use a stop-watch to time the relationship between demo and practice. In an exam, more than 1 minute of demonstration for every 3 of practice is an automatic fail. The students aren't there to listen to you; they are there to practice swordsmanship. If what you want them to do takes more than 2 minutes maximum to explain and show, then it is too complicated for the class you have in front of you. If they need to learn something academic, then by all means begin or end the class with a lecture, with the students seated, taking notes etc. But when they are standing in class, sword in hand, they need to be kept moving.

. . .

How should you demonstrate?

Demonstration is a critical skill for an instructor. You have to show them the drill exactly the way you want them to do it, with just enough verbal explanation that they know why they are doing it. So, show them the action, slowly and accurately. Then briefly, briefly, briefly explain it. Then show it to them again, one to four times, switching direction so they can see it from both sides. I quite often get asked to show the action again; I'll demonstrate it as often as I'm asked to. But I don't ask for questions. Students who need to ask a question to get the drill will do so whether I ask them to or not, so long as I have established the class environment such that they feel comfortable with me; and as I go round the class, they can ask their question without disrupting everyone else's practice.

If you need to sell them on the action, then do it hard and fast once with an experienced assistant, as the first demonstration. Do not screw this up! If needs be, while they are working on the previous drill, grab your assistant and go over what you'll want them to do. Then show the class exactly what you want them to do.

Show them exactly what you want them to do. Avoid advertising common errors. I learned this when I found a young student, whose English skills didn't quite catch which of the two possible versions he'd seen was the one I wanted him to do, faithfully copying the wrong one. Certainly not his fault!

Demonstration guidelines

- Show them exactly what you want them to do.
- Keep the roles the same; if you start out as the defender, stay that way until the end of the demonstration.
- Highlight the bit you want them to focus on, such as the footwork.

• Show it at the speed you want it done, or a bit slower. They will naturally speed up on their own.

• Focus on getting them to do it, not doing it yourself.

• If necessary, prepare the demonstration with your partner beforehand.

So, the time in each block will go something like this: 1-2 minutes of demonstration; 5-6 minutes of practice; possibly 1 minute of class correction, followed by 3 minutes practice. When in doubt, talk less. Only stop the class if you need to. So how do you know when you need to?

Class Progression

The class plan almost never survives intact. A question here, a problem there, and very soon you have taken 14 minutes for a ten minute block. You may have spotted that my example above might be 12 minutes long (2 min demo, 6 min practice, 1 min demo, 3 min practice). This is ok, so long as you don't try to compress the rest of the material into the time left. Take your time, and drop as much of your material as necessary. I have seen hundreds of class plans in my time, and I have never once seen one with insufficient material for the time allowed.

How do you know when to move on, or when you've gone too far and need the class to take a step back? In short, if everyone is busy training, leave them to it. If the flow starts to clog up, the class is either unready for the current assignment, so bring them back a step; or ready to move on, so add the next action or move on to the next drill.

The flow of the class is greatly affected by the level of difficulty. Too easy, and everyone gets bored, and stops. Too hard, and they get confused or frustrated, and stop. There is a sweet-spot where everyone is challenged but not overwhelmed, and you know they are there when everyone is busily engaged with the content you've set them. This is of course an application of the principle of Flow that I wrote about in *The Seven Principles of Mastery*.

Stopping the class

You should stop the class for one of the following reasons only:

1. Safety. If things are looking dangerous, stop.
2. Obvious error. If more than half the class is making the same mistake, stop and correct the group, rather than make individual corrections.
3. If the training flow is clogged either move onto something harder, or step back to something simpler.
4. Time: classes must finish on time. It is disrespectful to your class to keep them past the allotted time.

Familiar content, or new material?

What is the difference between setting the class a new, unfamiliar exercise, and setting them something that most of them know? In short, for new material, demonstrate step by step, and have them do each step before adding the next. Demo for 2 minutes, have them train for 4. For familiar stuff, demo for 1 minute or less, have them practice for 5.

If your class is struggling with the material, then take a step back. If they are having trouble with mechanics, the best solution is to give them an exercise that requires them to make the correction in a natural way. For example, if your style requires an upright stance, but the students are tending to lean forward, have them do footwork exercises with something balanced on their heads to keep them upright. Then ask them to focus on the feeling of being upright as they do it. Then have them recreate that feeling during the previous exercise that they were struggling with. If the problem is choreographical, then take them back a step or two in the drill. In every case, bring them back to a place where they can do the actions reasonably well, then build the difficulty back up.

I am working on the assumption, which may be flawed, that if you have been teaching for a short while, or are about to start, that you have a basic training in your style, and a comprehensive arsenal of drills and games to draw on for teaching it. If the class has a problem and you don't have the tools to fix it, then probably the best solution is to change the topic of the class to something else. Or you can cheat: present the class with the problem, and ask them to come up with ways of fixing it. Don't do this with beginners (unless the problem is very simple). I use this a lot, and it works very well at getting the students involved in the development of new drills and approaches.

The Different Kinds of Practice

The excellent Rory Miller talks about four different kinds of training in martial arts: teaching, training, operant conditioning, and play.

• Teaching, by which he means verbal explanation, is good for theory and background, but useless for teaching fast, hard, physical responses to actions.

• Training, by which he means repetition of known actions, in a low stress environment. This is better than nothing but is a very slow and insecure way to generate useful stress responses.

• Operant conditioning is hard to do well, but by far the most effective training tool for actual violence. It works by breaking the OODA loop. Let me explain: When stuff happens, you first Observe it, then Orient to it, then Decide what to do, then Act. All this takes time, and if your opponent has the initiative, you're dead. Operant conditioning takes "Orient" and "Decide" out of the loop, and reduces it to what is effectively an instinctive reaction. The way you do it is to set up the stimulus, and make it so that the desired response is instantly rewarded, and so learned. Any other response, including failing to respond, is instantly punished, and so avoided in future.

• Play. It is very effective training to set up games that reward the desired actions. In a lecture on the history of combat, it's 99% teaching, 1% play, and that's it. In a basic martial arts class though, it should be 5% teaching, 65% training, and 30% play, or thereabouts. Too much play and you lose the structure; not enough, and it becomes very ineffective. One of my most common exhortations in class is "got it? now play with it."

WHAT HAPPENS if there's an Accident?

Swordsmanship training is inherently dangerous. Accidents will happen. Your job is to make sure that they happen as little as possible. There is a fundamental difference between being responsible and being culpable. While students are under your care, you are responsible for their safety. Provided you stick to the syllabus and safety guidelines of your school or club and behave responsibly, you are not morally culpable even if you are the one responsible. (This is not legal advice: I am not a lawyer.)

Before class even starts, there should be at least the following things in place: a first aid kit (check it now!), someone present who is trained in first aid (ideally everyone who ever leads a class is so trained), and a working phone in case of an emergency.

What should you do if:

1) You see a student sitting out? Ask them what's wrong, help them if needed. They may just be tired, or may have been hit badly but did not want to make a fuss. Always check.

2) There is an accident? Stay calm. Depending on the severity: either apply first aid, apply first aid and organise a lift to the nearest Accident and Emergency room, or apply first aid and call an ambulance.

On a related note, I would say that it is immoral to teach any martial art that requires actions to be repeated that will generate injury over time even if done correctly. It's just not ok to have your students do things that will reliably create (for example) joint problems in the long term. Assuming that your style is fundamentally mechanically healthy, then it becomes your responsibility to make sure that the mechanics that you teach are sufficiently correct that they will not injure the student. The easiest way to reduce the likelihood of self-inflicted mechanical injury before your own skills are sufficient to teach actions correctly at a deep level, is to keep everything slow and gentle. The lower the forces involved, the less likely an injury is to occur, and the less severe it will be. In the long term though, you should be carefully studying the ergonomics of your style.

Three Common Problems in Class

1. Disruptive questions

You have a student asking too many derailing questions: Tell them to ask them after class. If they persist in talking too much, ask them privately not to. One student had this problem, so I bet him 50 push-ups he couldn't get to the end of class without talking. He won. I did the push-ups. He said "I get it", and the problem was solved.

. . .

2. Your students know more than you do

Of course it often happens that students may show up to class that have more experience than the person in charge, so how do you push people along who are already ahead of you? This is quite daunting for the inexperienced, but just remember your prime directive, and try some of these key phrases:

"Add a degree of freedom to that"

"Coach for the first two passes then do the drill competitively"

"How's your grounding?"

3. An unresponsive class

This can be hell. And it is especially difficult with a class of people you don't know. It is very easy to let yourself spiral out of control trying to get a reaction out of them. I suggest the following instead:

• Get them playing a game as a group. For example, the "glove game", which works in any style. The rules are: 1) everybody has to keep moving 2) throw two gloves into the class 3) students can pick up gloves from the floor, and have to hit other students on the back with them. If you are hit on the back, you're out. 4) anyone holding a glove can also be knocked out of the game by being tapped on the back with a hand. 5) if you're holding a glove and are knocked out, you throw the glove away. 6) if it's safe with your students, allow disarms.

• Get them to plan the class they want; gather them round in a circle and ask them what they want to learn or practise today.

• Don't take it personally. You're not an entertainer. If they don't want to be there, they can leave.

'Hopeless' Students

There are some people who find even the most basic actions or sequences incredibly difficult to learn. If you have someone like that in your class, here are some points to remember.

• They can walk and talk. These are both fantastically complicated skills. So they probably can learn swordsmanship. You just have to help them figure out how.

• Reduce complexity as far as possible. For example, give them sword exercises they can do standing still.

• If possible, assign a different senior student to help this person every time the class moves on.

• Keep rotating the class pairings, so that nobody gets stuck with them, and they don't feel like they are holding someone back.

• Praise their effort. Tell them that progress will come.

• Take a short video of them now, which nobody will look at yet, and another video of them doing the same exercise in three or six months' time. Watch the two clips side by side, together with the student, to give you both a clear sense of their progress. They will probably be amazed by the difference.

Aggressive or Unsafe students

They do exist, and it can be hard to get through to them that their behaviour is unacceptable. Let me remind you though of the prime directive. Your first and highest responsibility is to the well-being of your students. So you must be able to ask a person to sit out an exercise, or even leave the class. I have had many senior students with the physical competence to teach great classes, but whose promotion to teaching has been delayed while we worked on their ability to take command when necessary. Age can also be a factor; very young students (under 20) learning to run classes can find it especially hard to command older students. It is well worth modelling this situation (as you would model accidents in a first aid class), and actually practise asking a person to leave.

You will have the backing of your other students, because nobody wants to train with an unsafe person. If you have any doubts on this score, then appoint a back-up person, someone you trust, whose job in class is to back you up if you need to deal with a problematic student.

If this situation arises, do everything you can to let the person in question save face. Take them quietly aside and gently remonstrate; if that doesn't work, take them aside again and ask them to leave. Have your backup person standing next to you when you do it, but ideally, nobody else in class is even aware that someone has been expelled. Of course, if their actions have been obvious and public, then you need to face them down. But again, leave them their pride, and let them leave in peace.

Dojo **Busting**

Back in the bad old days of martial arts, "dojo busting" was quite common. People would go round challenging martial arts teachers to fight; if the teacher lost, all their students would leave them and join the school of the dojo buster. When I opened my school, I was concerned that it might happen to me, and I'd either kill someone or lose my school. It never did happen, and I've not heard of it happening in real life in the last 20 years. But I asked a senior Finnish martial arts teacher about it, and his answer was simple: if someone comes dojo busting, just ask them to leave. If they don't, then call the police. Good advice.

Defining **Success**

It only remains to define success. In order of importance, your basic class was successful if:

1. There are no injuries.
2. Everyone was busy

3. They ended class better martial artists than they started it
4. The theme goal was met.

TEACHING IS A SKILL. You learn it by doing. So get to work!

And next up, let's look at bringing the historical aspect of historical martial arts into your classes...

HOW TO GET THE BOOK INTO CLASS

Historical Martial Arts are distinct from other kinds of martial arts in that we base our art on historical sources. This means that the teacher is in effect a mediator between the student and the source or sources (The Book) that your art is based on. You should enable the students that want to work directly with The Book to do so. It is never too early in a student's training to introduce them to The Book. Here are the key elements of connecting the student to the source:

Put The Book on show

Have The Book there in the salle, and open to whatever page is most relevant to what you are doing in class. This is vital: so much so that I built a lectern especially to hold my sources when teaching in my home salle in Helsinki. A physical book is better than a screen, because it encourages students to touch it and turn the pages. Most people are understandably shy about fiddling about with someone else's laptop, but will happily flick through a book.

. . .

Connect actions to The Book

Regularly connect what you are doing in class with what's in the book. For instance, once I have taken a beginner's class through the first couple of blows (right shoulder, extended, to left hip; then return through the extended position and up to the shoulder) I show them *posta di donna destra, posta longa, dente di zenghiaro, mandritto fendente* and *roverso sottano* in the Getty Ms. This takes only a minute or two (don't go off on an academic side-track), but makes it really obvious where our actions are coming from, and connects the action to The Book. I tell my beginners that I live in mortal fear that somebody might one day leave one of my classes with the impression that I've made this all up.

Quote The Book

Whenever you are demonstrating an action from The Book, try to use the language from The Book. For instance, when I'm teaching Fiore's breaking the thrust, I might say:

"As Fiore tells us, step the front foot out of the way and pass across"

And

"As Fiore wrote, when you're breaking the thrust '*pigla cum il fendente*', "grab it with a fendente""

This way the students are continually connecting what we are doing with The Book.

It's ideal to use the original language every now and then for key phrases, but you should usually include a translation (such as when I'm teaching sword and buckler from I.33, I'll say "*ligans ligati contrarii sunt et irati. Fugit at partes laterum. Peto sequi.* The binder and the bound are contrary and irate. He flees to the side. I seek to follow"). This is no different from judo teachers teaching *ukemi* not 'falls'. How much of the original terminology you expect the students to learn is a matter of syllabus design, but especially if The Book isn't written in English, you as the teacher should be prepared to at least acknowledge that fact to the students. It's worth memorising a few key phrases to convey the flavour of what we are trying to do.

Using Translations

As a professional historical martial arts teacher I feel it's a matter of professional ethics to be able to work with my sources in their original languages. That's why I don't teach German martial arts, or Hungarian. You would expect a University professor of Russian Literature to be able to read Russian, right? But for unpaid teachers it's not reasonable to expect that level of academic depth, so you may be working from translations. That's fine, so long as that's made clear to the students, and you take a moment to explain that your understanding of the source is mediated through somebody else's translation. Keep a copy of that translation there with The Book (or use a combined edition) so that students can actually read it, and yes, check up on you...

Skin in the Game

When I show beginners The Book, I'll tell them that sometimes what we are doing in class is not exactly what's shown in the source. There can be three reasons for this:

1. I've made a mistake.

2. I have deliberately adapted the original technique for reasons that I can explain.

3. The student is mistaken in their interpretation.

Then I invite the students to catch me out, and tell them that sometimes I'll depart from the source deliberately *just to see if they are paying attention*. I'll also sometimes put some skin in the game: if they catch me in a mistake, I'll do 50 push-ups (or similar). This introduces a playful element, and really encourages the students to try to catch me out, which means they'll actually go check the source.

Departing from The Book

Of course, not everything you do in class is straight from The Book, but you need to be clear about what is direct from the source, what's been adapted, and what's been brought in from somewhere else. I'm a big fan of bringing in outside elements, but it has to be done carefully or you end up with a Frankenstein's monster of a system, with bits cobbled together that don't really fit.

For instance, the Getty Ludwig MS XV manuscript is my primary source when teaching *Armizare*, but when we are covering the third master of the dagger, I'll usually use the disarm as shown in the Pisani-Dossi manuscript. This is a very cool technique, but more importantly is a firm reminder that there is more than one version of the treatise.

In my rapier course and workbooks, which are based on my interpretation of Capoferro's art, I include a rapier and cloak technique from Alfieri. This reminds students that there is more than one source, and having gained a thorough grounding in one rapier style, they should absolutely work with other sources to gain a broader knowledge.

The key concept is transparency. It should be absolutely clear to every student that cares about historicity where what you are teaching them is coming from. And as the future of the art depends on students getting stuck into the research side of things, it's part of your remit to encourage and enable students to begin working with the sources.

Next up, let's look at how to teach an Advanced Class...

TEACHING AN ADVANCED CLASS

It sounds hard, right?

It really isn't. In an advanced class, the students already know the syllabus. You've already taught them the techniques and tactics for the system (or somebody else has). So it is all about developing skill. Here's the mantra: *advanced technique is basic technique done really well.*

Advanced students by definition must already know how to run a diagnostic, fix the weakest link, and run the diagnostic again (see the chapter Troubleshooting for more on diagnostics). So what is the instructor even there for?

1. You create an expectation of mindful practice. It is easier for them to stay focussed on what they should be working on if you are there holding the space for them.

2. If they get stuck, can't figure out how to fix a problem, or can't figure out what problem to fix, you can make useful suggestions.

3. If the class starts to flag, you can intervene to get things going again.

. . .

THAT'S REALLY IT. I usually begin an advanced class by gathering the students round and asking them my first question: "what are you working on?"

Answers may include dealing with fencers who rush in, getting hit on the hands when attacking, getting feints to work, stopping falling for feints, and so on.

Students at this level should already know where their weaknesses are, and have an idea what to do about them. Hearing each other's problems lets them organise into pairs, threes, or working solo, depending on what problems they are trying to fix. So my next question is "what are you going to do about it?" And each student in turn will tell me their plan, such as: set up a drill where my partner rushes in on me, or get my partner to snipe for my hands when I attack, and so on.

Then they go work on those things. After a while, I'll gather them round again and ask: "is that problem still the weakest link?"

The possible answers are:

1. Yes, but it's getting better. So carry on with what you were doing.
2. Yes, and it's not getting better. So change your approach.
3. No, so I've found another problem.
4. I don't know, so run the diagnostic again.

AND ROUND WE GO AGAIN.

It is very easy to incorporate your own training time into this kind of class, but keep an eye on the clock, and remember to check in with the whole class every 10-15 minutes.

Sound simple? It really is. Teaching individual lessons is much harder, and teaching beginners is hardest of all. It's sufficiently different that it gets its own chapter later in the book. Coming up next is how to teach a mixed level lesson...

TEACHING A MIXED-LEVEL CLASS

All classes are mixed level to some degree, including day one of the beginners' course. This is because some students will have relevant prior training, or be quicker to pick up choreography than others. There is no such thing as a homogenous class.

The trick is to set the level of the class such that the more experienced are sufficiently challenged, and the beginners are not overwhelmed. What this boils down to is managing the class in such a way that everyone is training at a useful level for them. Here's how I do it:

Mentally I divide the class into two or three groups: beginners, intermediates, and advanced (or any pair out of those three). This is based on how well they understand skill development, and is much less to do with their breadth of knowledge.

Advanced students can be told run a diagnostic, fix the weakest link, carry on, and they'll just get on with it.

Intermediate students can be shown a drill, and some variations, and told to go play with it.

Beginners need to be shown exactly what you want them to do.

I allow students to self-select their level within a class, by showing them what each group is about to do, and letting them choose which activity they feel ready for. More on this in a moment.

Whatever the mix of skill levels, the class always starts and ends with everyone together doing the same thing. It's important for their sense of being all part of the one school, all part of the one class, that they start and finish together.

I'll then have the advanced students teach the beginners or intermediates for a while, and keep swapping back and forth between the groups training with themselves, and one group coaching the other.

LET ME TAKE A CONCRETE EXAMPLE, and walk you through it with a class divided into two groups.

Topic: Longsword Mechanics (Fiore)

The ONE THING: Moving smoothly, connecting the sword to the hand. Students should be moving better at the end than they were at the beginning.

Time	Content
18.00	Welcome and warm-up, emphasise the swing, and connecting feet to hands
18.15	Standing step drill, connecting feet to hands
18.20	Four guards drill, connecting hands to feet. Lead with the hand!
18.25	The Stick Exercise. Keep moving!
18.30	First 7 plays first master of dagger. Plus counter. Emphasis on turning opponent's hips.
18.45	Sword handling: six grips, up down around around.
18.55	Cutting drill, parts one and two (class already knows it). Emphasis on continuous movement.
19.05	Farfalla di ferro, continuous movement
19.15	Variations on the breaking the thrust drill, emphasis on continuous movement
19.25	Revise part 2 cutting drill, especially breaking the thrust
19.30	Close.

The warm-up is done all together, though I'll throw in some advanced variations for the fitter members of the class. For instance, while one person is doing a slow squat then a slow push-up, another might be doing them smoothly together, while another is doing them with a jumping squat, while another is doing a full push-up-twisting-squat-jump-burpee (see the Syllabus Wiki if you don't know the exercise). This reinforces the message that all actions can be done at whatever level is useful to the student.

The standing step drill: I'll pair advanced with beginners, so the advanced students are basically teaching the drill to the beginners. After a few minutes I'll get them to change partners and practice with someone at close to their own level. This is one drill where size and strength really matter, so there may be smaller advanced students training with bigger beginners. The students self-select their partners based on size and experience.

The Four Guards drill: This is basic solo training. If we have anyone in class who doesn't know it, I'll assign one of the advanced students to walk them through it, while everyone else practices it at their level. Advanced students might be playing around with it— I'll only get them to stick exactly to the drill if their play is getting distracting to the beginners.

The Stick Exercise: the one with the stick is determining the level of difficulty for each person they swing the stick at. Advanced students get no second chances and are hunted down without mercy if they make the slightest mistake; beginners get a gentle introduction to the drill, and a few chances to get it right without penalties. So, the class is all doing the same thing, but at different levels.

The first 7 plays of the 1st master: I'll demonstrate all seven plays in order, and have the advanced students go play with them, while the beginners work through remembering the order. As soon as they have it, I'll get them to choose one to work on (or a play and its counter), and ask an advanced student to coach them in getting better at making it work. After they have been doing this for a little while, I may have the advanced students 'use' their beginner. (See the section on teaching beginners for details on how to use them.)

Sword handling drills: the whole class does these together. If a beginner is getting stuck I might assign an advanced student to model it for them.

The cutting drill parts one and two, farfalla di ferro: same process. These are solo drills, so everyone can go at their own pace. One student might be going through part one of the cutting drill while another plays with the whole cutting drill and the *farfalla* without pause.

Variations on the breaking the thrust: beginners may need to be taught the drill choreographically, so I'd start with that, while the advanced students play with the variations. Then have the advanced students pick a beginner to train, and teach or coach the basic action or whatever variations their beginner is ready for. As with the dagger plays, I might allow the advanced students to use their beginner once they have helped them along a bit first.

Revise part two of the cutting drill: this includes breaking the thrust from *posta di donna la sinestra,* and using *bicorno* to defeat the break with a feint. The beginners may or may not be ready for this — they can stick to the basic version of the drill, or learn the choreography of this new way of doing the break, or if they already know it, coach one side of the action or the other. Use the advanced students to teach the new action only after they have had a chance to play with it.

We will probably find that there is too much material here for the mixed level group, because they have to keep changing partners. That's fine— just drop some of the material, and emphasise that which is most likely to communicate the ONE THING.

As you can imagine, a student might fit into the beginners' group if they don't know the cutting drill version of the break, but be in the advanced group when it comes to the dagger plays. This is why I let them self-select, and allow movement between the groups. If this is done well, then every student finishes the class having improved their skill, perhaps broadened their knowledge, and been useful to their peers, either as a coach, or as a training partner, or both. No beginner has been dropped in the deep end, and no advanced student has spent all of their precious class time walking beginners through basic actions.

One thing to watch for though is to avoid selecting the same advanced student to help out too often (unless they are interested in being trained to teach). Coaching is one of the fundamental skills of becoming a good martial artist; it's the foundation of all skill development. So make sure all your advanced students get the opportunity to practice coaching.

If the class is large enough, and the skill differential broad enough, then it may be useful to have a middle group, the intermediates, who act as 'advanced' students to the beginners, and as beginners with the advanced students. This gives the advanced students more time to work at their own level, and more advanced students to coach when it's their turn to help out. But, working with real beginners is a skill in itself, so even in a three-level class I'll usually work in at least one segment where the advanced students coach the beginners.

You may have a very small group of advanced students in a sea of beginners. In that case, during the segments where the advanced students are coaching beginners, some beginners will be working with each other instead. That's not a problem. Likewise if you have just a few beginners: while they are getting coaching from the advanced students, most of the advanced students will be paired off with each other.

TEACHING A BEGINNERS' COURSE

Beginners are the future of every art, and the lifeblood of every school. Teaching beginners is a holy terror and a privilege. You only get one chance at a first impression, so I have only one clear shot to give a new student a clear and honest impression of the Art as I see it. If I do my job properly and they decide it's not for them, then they are basing that on an accurate idea of what they are rejecting. That's fine. What keeps me up at night before teaching a beginners' course is the idea that I might misrepresent the art, and lose a student to the Art who would actually have stuck with it if I'd only done my job properly.

Because it is so high-stress, I recommend getting plenty of experience teaching regular classes before running a beginners' course. If that is not an option, then make sure you have read and internalised my guidelines for teaching a basic class before you plan out and teach your beginners' course.

How a club treats beginners is a defining feature of its culture. In my schools, beginners are considered the future of the art and welcomed accordingly. In general, clubs either run beginners' courses or expect beginners to just show up to a class. I ran my school without formal beginners' courses for the first year and a half, and it doubled in size when we ran the first beginners' course. Most beginners just don't feel comfortable showing up unless they know that they are expected, and expected to be inexperienced.

I run my beginners courses with two rules and four principles.

The Rules:

1. Every student must finish every class healthier than they started it.

This is accomplished by:

2. Every student must behave like a reasonable adult (whether they are adult, or reasonable, outside the salle or not).

The Principles

1. **Funnels not filters**

Beginners' courses should be funnels, not filters. They should entice people in and seduce them to the art, not hold up artificial barriers to entry (such as the push-ups-till-you-puke approach). A beginners' course is either a filter or a funnel. A club that is trying to produce competition champions will usually try to filter out students that will never do well in competition. They do this by making the beginners' course a selection procedure, requiring a certain level of grit or fitness to get through. That's perfectly legitimate behaviour; special forces units do the same. But if your club is run as an open learning environment, interested in progress rather than attaining a specific goal, a funnel makes more sense. Your purpose then is to equip students to take part safely in regular classes.

2. **Movement**

Get them moving: movement is the foundation of swordsmanship. Good movements create good guards, good blows, and so on. This starts with the warm-up and continues throughout the class.

3. **Start with what they can do**

Start with what they can do, and then adjust that towards what you want them to do. Every action must be taught from the familiar: walking across the salle becomes passing steps; swinging the sword from shoulder to shoulder becomes striking; and so on. If your art has passing steps, start with having them walk. If your art has lunges, start with having them reach out their arm for something. If it's a bit too far away, they'll shift their front foot naturally. Then take this natural action and modify it in the desired direction.

4. **The rule of beginners**

Show it to them correctly a thousand times, and they will eventually get it. Show it to them wrong once, and they'll copy it accurately first time.

Planning the course

When you plan your beginners course, you need to know two things:

1. How much time do you have? One three-hour session? Eight 90 minute classes, once a week for eight weeks?

2. What are you training them for? To be able to join regular classes safely, or some other goal?

Answering these questions will tell you what you need to cover, and in how much depth. The key thing to remember is that in any one session you will really only be able to teach them one thing. If you have just one induction class, that one thing should be how to train safely. So, what is the minimum amount of material they need to know to be able to join in with the regular classes?

It is worth remembering that no class plan survives first contact with the students (assuming you're actually paying attention to your class, that is), so don't stress the plan too much, just be clear about your goal, and the amount of time you have. Top tip: teach less, but teach it better.

For a thorough example of a beginners course plan for eight 90 minute classes, see my *Armizare Workbook Part One: Beginner's Course.* I have also documented a couple of beginners' courses on my blog at guywindsor.net. But be advised— I have been teaching for a long time, and so I can get more stuff into the students in less time. There is probably twice as much content in the workbook than you should aim for.

It's also useful to remember that every cohort is different. One group of beginners may be able to absorb twice as much as another cohort. It's impossible to know in advance before they show up, because it's not just a question of the individuals concerned, it's got a lot to do with how they interact with each other.

So, given the time you have, print out as many of the Beginners' course class plan handouts as you need to plan each session, and use the After Action Review from the first session to adjust the plan for the second one, and so on. Remember for beginners especially, the rule of teaching only ONE THING is especially true. Here's how I might think of my ONE THING for each of the eight sessions.

1. Historical Martial Arts are awesome, and you can really do it.
2. Mechanics matter
3. This is how we train each other (e.g. Rule of Cs)
4. Controlling the weapon (mine and my opponent's)
5. Footwork matters
6. Advanced technique is basic technique done really well, so let's improve the basics
7. Countering the defence

8. This is a single coherent system. We've looked at the very basics, but there is a world more cool stuff to learn.

It's your job above all to see them through the course safely. They probably have no experience of weapons handling or other martial arts training, so will need to be taught everything. It is *much better* to lose a student because they quit because of all the stooopid safety rules, than because they got injured.

So you have a bunch of beginners. How do you get your own training done when those around you are so much less experienced? That's next...

USING BEGINNERS

As we have seen, beginners are the future of any martial art. And the best learning environment is when you are the least knowledgable person in the room. Anyone you train with can teach you something. It is more difficult to keep learning when you are surrounded by relative beginners. When I moved to Finland in 2001, I was by a mile the most experienced practitioner of Historical Martial Arts in the country. Literally everyone I crossed longswords with knew less about the subject than I did. This could easily have lead to stagnation, but I managed to keep learning through the following ways:

- I cross-trained 3-4 times a week with other martial arts, one-on-one with senior instructors— basically trading classes. The potential for contaminating my interpretation was huge, but the upside was I developed a lot as a martial artist.
- I travelled a lot to international events, paying for it by teaching classes there. I treated these trips mostly as recruitment: when I saw an instructor I thought I and my students could learn from, I hired them over to teach seminars. We averaged three or four such seminars a year.

• I learned how to train usefully with beginners.

The last step is the critical one here. I will summarise the approach below for students about to work with beginners, then describe the class step-by-step as a potential class plan for instructors facing this perennial problem.

1. As we saw above the rule of beginners is this: show it to them right a thousand times, and they will eventually copy it correctly. Show it to them wrong once, and they will copy it perfectly first time. (I mean no disrespect. This is just true, and I've never seen a beginner for whom it wasn't.) So having beginners around demands that your every action is as perfect as you can make it. No pressure then.

2. Use the drill for your own purposes. One of the things beginners have to learn eventually is the terminology of the art. So on the beginners course we do things like call out the names of the steps (*accrescere, discrescere, passare, tornare,* etc.) and they have to do the named step. For more experienced students in the same class this could be unimaginably tedious, but should not be: they are expected to work at their own level. So while they are all doing the same thing, some are working on remembering the terms; some working on perfecting its mechanics; and some are working through possible applications, from power generation, to avoidance, to specific plays.

3. In pair drills, the beginner will naturally get parts of it wrong. Excellent. A genuine randomiser! The attack may be too strong, too far away, too close, in the wrong line, anything. And of course your job is to effortlessly and spontaneously adapt the drill to the specific conditions of the attack you get, not the one you expect. This demands 100% focus on what is happening. And when it is your turn to do what they just attempted, you have to demonstrate it perfectly according to the drill, of course. Your training alternates between 100% perfect tactical choices in real

time, and 100% perfect mechanics in your own time. Sounds like 100% perfect training, no?

YOU SHOULD ALSO NOTE the following:

• The attack is never "wrong": you get hit because you failed to defend. But the attack can always be improved.

• Your correction of the attack will be much more convincing if it comes after the attack has failed, than if you just got hit.

• Coach by modelling, not explaining. Beginners are not stupid, they are just unskilled. They need opportunities to practise, not a lecture.

• This kind of training demands 100% focus on the specifics of the attack that you get, not the one you expect.

• When training with beginners, you have an opportunity to go deep, making a few actions better. But you have less chance to go wide, using a broader range of actions (because this will bewilder the already overwhelmed beginner). When paired with more experienced students, you could take the chance to go wide if it doesn't conflict with the overall class goals.

So relish the influx of new perfection-demanding random generators, and relish the fact that in a decade or two, they may well be vastly better at this than you are now, but will always remember and be grateful for the help you gave them when they were starting out. You may be helping to train the next Bruce Lee, or Aldo Nadi, or even Fiore dei Liberi.

PART IV
TEACHING INDIVIDUALS

TEACHING THE INDIVIDUAL LESSON

The individual lesson is just a formalised way of doing the usual pair training. The coach should create an environment in which the desired behaviour results in the student striking, and undesired behaviour results in the student being struck.

You don't have to be technically superior to your students to run a good class, but you do need a high level of skill to give a good individual lesson. Coaching requires the highest levels of technical skill because you have to be in sufficient control of the situation that you allow yourself to be hit when the student has done what you want, but whenever their action is undesired, it must fail and you must strike. This way the student learns very, very, fast, as the environment they are in makes learning and improving absolutely natural.

As you already know, every drill from day one can be practiced according to the Rule of Cs, so every student should be learning how to generate the optimal rate of failure in their training partners from day one. I introduce it so early because it is a high level skill that takes a long time to master, so we should start that time as early as possible. This means that if you have been training properly *you are already an experienced coach.*

But there is something of a mindset shift when you are not trading coaching back and forth, but are THE TEACHER. Those caps are entirely in your own head, but the phenomenon is real, so let's build up to this skill in stages.

Verbal correction of a solo drill

The student does one iteration of a solo drill; you watch it and make one verbal correction, with as few words as possible. The student then repeats the drill, applying the correction. See if it makes an improvement. Use simple words, and avoid statements of judgement ('good', 'bad' etc.) until the end of the lesson, then praise the student for their effort, and acknowledge any improvement they have made. The one context in which verbal correction is your only real option is when teaching online.

Prescribe a drill to improve a solo drill

The same set-up as above, but this time the coach had to prescribe a specific exercise to be done, either solo or with the coach, to improve the solo drill, with a second iteration of the solo drill to see whether the coach's prescription worked.

Improve one step of a specific pair drill

Take a basic drill and improve your student's execution of one step of it. Set it up so if the action is improving, the student succeeds, if not, then they fail. Adjust the difficulty level such that the student usually succeeds, but only by working at their upper limit. Optimal rate of failure, always.

For example, a drill beginning with a simple attack from wide measure. The trick is to get it better and better, and faster and faster, by having the student beat the coach's parry. The parry should be done such that it creates a closing window, that the attack should just sneak through.

This is the bare bones of how to coach, but you can apply this kind of approach to any class situation where you are a student. You don't have to be giving individual lessons all the time to learn how to do it. Any time you are paired off with a student of lower skill, make it your aim to raise your partner's skill level without actually giving them a formal lesson— just subtly modify what you do so that they naturally improve. (This is high level stuff!)

How to give a short technical lesson (6-7 minutes, plenty of time to create a clear improvement):

1. Identify or illustrate a technical problem (the right action done insufficiently well)

2. Set up a drill in which the student has to perform the action at increasing levels of intensity

3. Adjust the intensity to generate the optimum rate of failure

4. Assess the results. If good, go to step 5, if not good go back to step 2 and change the drill.

5. Keep increasing the pressure under which the student performs the improved action, so their rate of failure stays the same while their skills improve.

How to give a short tactical lesson.

1. Identify or illustrate a tactical problem (the wrong action is being done)

2. Set up a drill in which the student has to select the right action at increasing levels of intensity

3. Adjust the intensity to generate the optimum rate of failure

4. Assess the results. If good, go to step 5, if not good go back to step 2 and change the drill.

5. Keep increasing the pressure under which the student selects the correct action, so their rate of failure stays the same while their skills improve.

Now it may seem that I just copied and pasted all of that, but that's not actually true. The thing is, the basic process of running an individual lesson is always the same. The specific content may change, but the pattern and the process is always the same.

This begs the question of how can you react in time to a student's error to give the necessary physical feedback? Basically, if you can't see the student's error in time, you can't give the lesson. So, either slow the lesson down, to give you more time, or learn to read the error earlier in the student's action. This is where experience comes in— but if you deliberately set out to gain that experience, you will pick it up quite quickly.

A video example may be useful here, so you can watch me giving Dave Smith a Sword and Buckler lesson on video here: https://guywindsor.net/SandBlesson

LET'S take a deeper dive into skill development, and look at how to prepare students for freeplay, and use freeplay as a training tool. That's next…

PART V
SKILL DEVELOPMENT

SKILL DEVELOPMENT

The most critical factor in skill development is deliberate practice. There is nothing wrong with messing about and blowing off steam with a bit of sword related fun. But the key thing to teach your students from the beginning is *how to practice.* There is only one effective pattern to practice, and it's this: run a diagnostic, fix the weakest link, run the diagnostic again. So at any stage of their development, no matter what kind of training they are doing, the student should know exactly what it is they are trying to accomplish, and it should always be solving a problem that they have experienced.

In the beginning, you as the teacher will be running a diagnostic drill to see what your students need next, then deciding which aspect of their art is the weakest link, prescribing specific training practices to strengthen that link, and then checking to see whether it's worked. This process should be transparent to the student, because as soon as possible you want them to be running their own diagnostics and fixing their own weakest links. I start teaching them this in the first few classes they attend. As soon as they have (for example) two or more dagger techniques to practice, they can run through them quickly, and choose one to concentrate on.

The weakest link may be something they know, but can't do well, or something they don't know. In other words, they may need to work on depth, or breadth. It is relatively easy to teach set drills to a student or class, and therefore relatively easy to add breadth. There is always something new or different you could add.

It is much more demanding to add depth: to develop real skill in your students.

The key to this process is training at the optimal rate of failure, as determined by a clear, objective, and immediate feedback mechanism. Such as getting hit. The optimal rate of failure is generated by adding either complexity, or intensity, or both. This is why we train all drills, from the very beginning, according to the Rule of Cs. This acts as a multiplier, in that it can create many variations of any basic drill.

The "Rule of Cs"

The "Rule of Cs" describes the three fundamental ways in which a drill can be practiced: choreography, coaching, competition.

1. Choreography: the students co-operate in creating the correct choreography of the drill. This is where just about every set drill starts.

2. Coaching: Once the choreography is smooth, we choose one part of it, and have one student coach the other in that part, by adjusting the difficulty to create the optimal rate of failure. This is the heart of the process of skill development, so I'll expand on it at length in a moment.

3. Competition: The players each try within reason to make the drill work for them. This can be dangerous, so be careful, and have

the students wear full protection just in case. In practice, the more experienced fencer should get most of the hits, without departing from the drill. This is fine, and gives a good indication of whether your training regime is working.

There is a significant risk of this getting out of hand so keep a careful watch. Make sure that they stick to the constraints of the drill that you have set. Otherwise they will lose track of the rationale behind what they are doing, and mistakes creep in that are difficult to spot and to trace back to their source, and of course there may be an accident. We will go into competitive training in more detail later, but for now let's take a look at coaching, which is simply the process of generating the optimal rate of failure in your training partner or students. For now let's assume we're doing an ordinary sword drill, in which the optimal rate of failure will be somewhere around 20-30%.

As the *rate* of failure is so important, we need to be able to adjust the complexity and intensity very precisely. Let's start with a diagnostic drill for breadth.

Most drills look something like this:

1. Attacker and Defender are ready to go.
2. Attacker attacks with action A
3. Defender defends with action B
4. Attacker continues with action C
5. Defender counters C with action D

and so on. Let's call this drill ABCD. Action A is the tactical context for defence B. The easiest way to start expanding on this drill is to add breadth by working the combinations, like so:

1. Set up the drill ABCD. Then, from the same starting point, whatever that is in your system, the Attacker varies their attack; actions A2, A3, A4, and so on. Be that "thrust from the left", "beat attack and lunge in quarte", "go for the hip throw", or whatever. In each case, the defender should make the proper defence.

2. The next stage is for the Attacker to use whichever attack

they have chosen to set up their counter; A draws B, so they can do C.

3. Then of course, the Attacker does A-C so the Defender can practice D.

4. In most systems, attack A has more than one defence; so once you have worked through all the main attacks, go back to one of them, and work through all the main defences against it. (My longsword students know this as the Four Corners Drill.)

5. Then work through the defences to all the main attacks.

6. Then do the same for the Attacker's counter to each of the defences generated by each of their attacks.

7. Then do the same for the Defender's counter to each of those...

This generates a combinatorial explosion. Very quickly, you could end up with a ridiculously complicated set of useless drills. So rather than writing up each of these new combinations as a set drill to memorise, you can teach this approach to your students as a way of surveying the system, to find where they have gaps in their knowledge. In effect, it's a diagnostic drill for breadth.

This is where many schools get stuck; they can get this far easily enough, and it generates all sorts of cool new sequences for students to remember, but doesn't really help them develop workable skills. The point of using multipliers is to avoid having to memorise too many sequences, so you can spend more time on skill development.

Teaching your students to coach each other

The key to teaching your students to coach each other is to introduce it early, in as simple a form as possible, so it becomes a natural part of training. In an Armizare beginners course, the first coaching exercise the students are likely to encounter is right after their first choreographical introduction to the first technique they learn from the manuscript: the first play of the first master of the dagger. In the basic drill, the attacker strikes with a mandritto, and the defender does a simple disarm. This usually means the defender stands there and tries to figure it out, while the attacker stands there and waits for them to get on with it. It's obvious to everyone involved that this is highly unnatural. But rather than teach the attacker to counter the technique, we just get them to continue in such a way that it forces the defender to keep moving.

Simply, the attacker enters with their mandritto, slowly and smoothly, and continues without pause reaching forward with their other hand to touch the defender's mask. So, the attacker adds an extension of the other hand and a pass. It's clear that if they could put their hand on your face, they could do much worse things. So the game becomes for the defender to do their action *and keep their face untouched.*

The attacker's job becomes to move at the speed at which the defender succeeds (i.e. does the disarm and doesn't get touched) at the optimal rate. You can see this drill at guywindsor.net/aw1006.

By keeping it so simple, beginners in their first class are already able to meaningfully coach each other, and it is extraordinary to watch how quickly the defenders get better at doing the basic action.

Another simple way to introduce coaching skills to your students early is the Buckler Game (see the chapter The Model), in which the coach is very obviously defined as the one with the buckler, and it takes very little technical skill for the coach to generate the optimal rate of failure.

By including these kinds of exercises from the beginning, your students will learn how to coach each other, and treat it as a normal part of training. This is the secret sauce to skill development. As their technical skill increases, they will need ways of adapting the basic drills in a systematic and approachable way, to generate the optimal rate of failure in their training partners. We have already looked at specific variation multipliers, such as going through every type of blow and defending against them. We also have a set of "multipliers", in addition to the Rule of Cs. They are:

1. Who moves first?
2. Adding a step
3. Adding degrees of freedom, so either partner gets one or more decision points.

1. Who Moves First?

In any set drill, you can

1. start the drill with both players standing still in guard (this is the usual set-up for beginners to start with)

2. change who attacks

3. draw the attack by some prior movement or invitation.

The great thing about this multiplier is it breaks the students' dependency on a fixed starting position. Flow drills (such as my dagger disarm flowdrill) have a similar effect.

In my salle we often start our drills from way out of measure. The trick is to arrive at the right time, in the right place, to do the initial actions of a particular drill, without exposing yourself. This is very hard, at the beginning.

But we are still stuck in an artificially short sequence of maximum four steps, so:

2. Add a Step

Another simple means to make a drill more useful is to allow the "loser" to counter the last step if they can. So for instance, you set up the drill, and, as the attacker counters, the defender may, if they see it coming and can think up something useful to do, counter the attacker's action. There is in theory no end to this drill, as every action can be countered. Adding one step at a time is good, or you can allow a kind of slow freeplay to develop.

3. Degrees of Freedom

At any stage in any drill, a set of decisions have been made. Systematically allowing a different choice to be made by one player, on the fly, introduces an element of unpredictability for the other player. For example, we might allow the attacker to choose their counter to the defence at random. This can be either to develop the attacker's decision-making skills (so the defender is helping them), or to develop the defender's ability to adapt (so the attacker is helping the defender). When there is a choice like that to be made, we say there is a degree of freedom—the attacker in this case has one degree of freedom—one point in the drill where they get to make a choice. The other player has to respond appropriately in real time. By adding degrees of freedom one at a time, we can get all the way from set drill ABCD to freeplay. Common places to add a degree of freedom are:

- The defender doesn't have to wait for the attack, but can preemptively attack.
- The attacker can vary the type of attack.
- The defender can vary the type of defence (the most common change is from parry-riposte (two motions, one to defend, one to strike) to counterattack (defence and strike in one motion).
- The attacker can vary their reaction to the defence (e.g. feint, or parry the riposte, or enter on the parry, etc.)

As the complexity of the training develops, mistakes will occur — that's the point. To learn from them, you (the teacher) have to know what just happened, and ideally the students will know too. This requires a good fencing memory, which can and should be trained for.

. . .

The Fencing Memory Drill

Most fencers start with zero memory for the phrases of a bout. This makes it very difficult for them to learn from their mistakes—if you don't know what happened, how do you change it? As with every skill, it will get better if you practice it deliberately. As you might have guessed, I have a drill for which the "one thing" is developing fencing memory.

This drill works best with three students: an attacker, a defender, and an observer. Switch roles after each phrase, to develop their ability to remember phrases they have both done and seen.

- Designate an attacker and a defender.
- Allow free choice of attack and defence, but no continuations (attacker can't counter).
- Attacker attacks as they like, defender tries to defend. Notice who gets hit.
- First one, then the other, describes in clear fencing language, in detail exactly what occurred.

For example: "Mary was in coda longa, I was in posta di donna. Mary attacked with a thrust to my face. I tried to exchange the thrust, but my sword caught on the back of my mask and I missed my parry. Mary's thrust landed in my face". Then Mary describes what she thought happened "well, I started in tutta porta di ferro, and attacked with a mandritto fendente ... (you'll be amazed how rarely they'll agree with each other to start with). Lastly, the observer states what they thought happened. If the observer doesn't have a reliable fencing memory yet, use a video camera too.

When one attack and one defence can be reliably described and repeated, add the attacker's counter. When that is easily recalled, then the defender can counter that, and so on. Once you have built it up so that your students can accurately reproduce a phrase of at least six actions (three from each side), their memory is ready for useful freeplay.

Pressure Drills

We should also take a look using Pressure Drills, which are exercises whose specific function is to get the students used to performing under, you guessed it, pressure. This adds intensity.

The most basic set-up has three students, all in full freeplay gear, whatever that is for your school or system. One student goes in the middle, and each of their two partners alternately deliver the same attack 10 times each. The one in the middle will defend against each attack as best they can. In theory, they will do the same technique perfectly 20 times. The attackers' job is to keep the one in the middle moving, keep them under pressure. They do not wait for the defender to sort themselves out after each action; as soon as the first defence is done, the next attack comes in. That's why there are two partners. As fatigue sets in, they will tend to make mistakes and get sloppy. Ideally, they will find it really, really hard to defend themselves.

The next level has the attackers varying their attacks; one from the left with a cut and the other with a thrust, for example; and the defender has to do two different defences correctly.

Then the attackers can attack as they please, their only job to keep the defender working under pressure.

Of course, in whichever set-up, immediately after one student was in the middle, they take one of the attacking roles, then the other, so on the fourth round, they're back in the middle again. Good luck.

It's an age-old secret of martial training that acute fatigue is a good mimic of combat stress. When your heart rate is up above 180 and your legs and arms feel like they are falling off, and you can still get your actions right, then you have truly learned something. But fatigue creates mistakes, which can be dangerous. As the instructor, it's your job to rein things in or call a halt before the pressure gets too much for safe training.

In summary, you as the teacher will run a diagnostic on your class to decide what to teach them next (this is often done from one class to another, so the last session determines the class plan for the next session). You will then set them some training activity, and watch as they do it.

As soon as any new choreography is reasonably fluent, you will assign one side of the drill to train the other— for example, the attacker is training the defender to do the defence better.

You may give precise instructions to the attackers as to how to do that— do they increase their speed? Or vary their starting point? How exactly would you like them to make the defender's lives harder without putting anyone at risk? Or in a more experienced group you may let the attackers choose how to vary the intensity or complexity to get the optimal rate of failure.

Again depending on the group you might allow them to drill competitively, which is only useful when they are quite close in skill level: a senior competing with a junior is boring for one and frustrating for the other. Refer to the Teaching a Mixed-Level Class chapter for advice on handling this.

You might then change the roles, so the defender is training the attacker, or move on to the next part of your class plan, depending on what you think is most useful right now.

Let's have a look at a couple of concrete examples of taking an action from the treatise, establishing the choreography, then working our way up to being able to apply that skill under pressure.

"The Exchange of Thrusts" goes through this process with Fiore's exchange of thrusts with the longsword; "The Parry Riposte in One Tempo" goes through this process with the equivalent technique from Capoferro: his parry-riposte in one tempo with the rapier. Feel free to skip one or the other if you're not interested in that weapon— the process is very similar for both actions. If you're not familiar with either Fiore or Capoferro's systems and you'd like me to work up an example in a system you do know, email me at guy@guywindsor.com with the details and I'll be happy to do so.

FIORE'S EXCHANGE OF THRUSTS AS AN EXAMPLE OF SKILL DEVELOPMENT

The *scambiare di punte* or exchange of thrusts is a foundational play in Fiore's *Il Fior di Battaglia,* in which you defend against a thrust by counter-thrusting in the same tempo. Let's take a look at how we can create the basic drill from the text, then gradually train the students to apply the technique in more demanding circumstances. I should point out that you would not normally cover this whole process in a single session, unless you are working with quite advanced students from a different style (who are unfamiliar with this specific play). Most beginners will take a couple of years or more to get to the most advanced stages of this process.

Remember that *every* stage of this process should be trained according to the Rule of C's (choreography, coaching, competition): once the choreography is understood, the students coach each other, and where appropriate compete to make their action work. This is why it takes so long! We are looking for skill, not just knowledge, and that takes time.

Also, the order is not precise; depending on the students, I may add the counter earlier, or add a step at the beginning earlier, and so on. This is just one way to do it.

I covered the basic action in detail in *From Medieval Manuscript to Modern Practice: the longsword techniques of Fiore dei Liberi*. My translation of Fiore's instructions for this play is:

> This play is called the exchange of thrust, and it is done like this, thus. When one strikes a thrust at you immediately advance your foot that is in front out of the way and with the other foot pass also out of the way, crossing his sword with with your arms low and with the point of your sword up in the face or in the chest as is pictured.

At this stage we should remember that Fiore loves us and wants us to be happy. He understands that sometimes one might miss a stroke, and that's OK. Because this action continues in the tenth play:

> From this exchange of thrust that is before me, comes this play, that immediately that the scholar that is before me does not place the thrust in the player's face, and leaves it such that he doesn't place it neither in the face nor the chest, and because perhaps the player was in armour, the scholar must immediately pass forwards with the left foot, and in this way must grab. And put his sword to work with good strikes, because the player's sword has been grabbed and he cannot get away.

So having missed our thrust, perhaps because the opponent is in armour, we pass again, grabbing the sword and striking. In practice I always teach these plays together, and you should continue with the grab whether you hit the face with the exchange or not. That way if you do miss, you'll continue without pause.

You can see the action on video at https://guywindsor.net/lszl009

Okay, so that's the basic set-up. So how do we teach the action, and how do we develop the core skill that the action represents? Let's have a look.

The basic drill (adapted from p. 111 of *The Medieval Longsword*, and assuming two right-handed fencers)

1. Wait in tutta porta di ferro, attacker in the same guard.
2. Attacker thrusts to your belly
3. Pick up your point and cross their sword (middle to middle, edge to flat), hands stay low
4. Step your front (left) foot out of the way (to the left—this pushes their point further away from you)
5. And pass across (so, diagonally left), thrusting to their face
6. Reach over your sword with your left hand and grab their sword by the handle
7. While passing with your left foot
8. And turn to your right with a *tutta volta*, keeping your point in their face.

The prerequisites:

To learn this play in its basic form, the students must know:

1. Basic safe training practices (control, use of masks, etc.) though you may teach them safe pair practice with this drill if it is the first pair drill with swords that you are teaching them
2. Thrusting
3. Tutta porta di ferro
4. The acrescere fora di strada, passo ala traversa footwork combination
5. The pass

6. The tutta volta.

So far, so good. This is basic choreographical stuff, so as soon as the choreography is reasonably solid let's have the attacker start training the defender to make the exchange, assuming the students are able to add a bit of intensity without adding significant risk. This will depend on their current level of training and the available equipment.

Once the action is fluent enough, we could look at doing the same action from a different guard. Which would be the best? I'd say *fenestra,* because Fiore wrote (on f26v of the Getty Ms):

> This is the window guard (*posta di fenestra),* which is always quick with malice and deceit. And it is mistress of covers and strikes. And it argues with all the guards, both high and low. And it often goes from one guard to another to deceive the companion. It places great thrusts and knows to break and exchange, these plays it can do well.

So, the best strike from here is the thrust, and you can do the exchange and the break from here. It makes sense then to do the drill with both students in fenestra, and see how that goes. You will probably find that their rear-weighted guards are less fluent than their forward weighted guards, so you may digress into the mechanics of rear-weighted guards.

The new prerequisites for doing the drill this way are the basic version of the drill, and fenestra.

This would be a good time to cover the idea that you should aim your thrust at the level of the sword. What target is exposed if you thrust at the belly of someone who is in fenestra? You can have the students see it for themselves (just make sure that if they are striking at hands or wrists, the one being struck has adequate protection or they are both moving very slowly).

Vary the starting point: Now that they have two basic ways to do the drill, in which the primary variation is the defender's guard position, they could try to make the drill work from all the guards that the defender knows.

Adding the counter: at some point you need to teach them at least one counter. Generally speaking we teach students to counter an action before we can teach them to prevent it, because prevention requires more advanced knowledge of the tactical prerequisites. So, how do we counter the exchange? The simplest option is to yield to a pommel strike.

Notice that with this action I am adding the counter much later than with the other basic drills in the syllabus. You may well choose to add it immediately after the students have grasped the basic choreography.

This creates a three step drill: attack, defence, counter to the defence. (I cover creating drills in depth in section 7, Syllabus Design.) You could of course keep adding counters, but my next move here would be to use 'who moves first' and/or 'add a step' to create a bit of context.

'Who moves first?' At this stage we still have a completely static set-up. The defender is waiting in a static guard, the attacker attacks from a static guard. This is highly unnatural, so let's play with it by getting the defender to move first.

Generally speaking, it's best to vary one side of the drill at a time, so let's have the attacker standing still in tutta porta di ferro (or fenestra), and the defender starting one passing step back out of measure, with the sword chambered on their left. The defender then enters into measure with a roverso fendente towards tutta porta di ferro. The attacker uses that tempo to enter with the thrust, so the defender has to do the exchange by reversing their blow.

Get this working choreographically, then have the attacker train the defender to respond to a 'surprise' attack with the exchange. The drill can be played to up to four steps (attack, defence, counter, counter to the counter).

Once this is comfortable, you could have both students starting out of measure, and approaching each other as they might in a fencing match; for *Armizare* practitioners, that would be with blows from guard to guard. At first their goal is to co-operate in creating the basic drill, but as soon as that's working, the defender is looking to set up the attacker with a realistic opportunity to enter with a thrust onto the defender's prepared exchange.

The Exchange in other contexts: this action should work whenever a thrust enters on the inside line and you don't have to beat it across the centre. It has been done so far only as the defence against an attack, so let's look at setting it up as a counter-riposte, where the initial attacker sets up the defender to riposte with a thrust, and then exchanges. One simple way to do this is to take First Drill from my longsword syllabus, and have the attacker counter the riposte (a thrust to the chest) with the exchange.

(If you're unfamiliar with my First Drill, see here: https://guywindsor.net/lszlfirstdrill)

. . .

How else can you draw a thrust onto your prepared exchange? I'm sure you can think of a few ways....

Preventing and countering

We already have one basic counter to the exchange. How else could we deal with it? We could work on the attack defeating the exchange, for example by using *bicorno* to prevent the exchange from working. In this case, the attacker will appear to be vulnerable to the exchange, but adjust their grip to make the exchange fail. If you are unfamiliar with my interpretation of *bicorno*, you can find it in *From Medieval Manuscript to Modern Practice: the longsword techniques of Fiore dei Liberi.*

As always, once the choreography is understood, play with it with all of the previous variations.

What would happen if your feint drew an exchange? Well, you could parry on the same side, parry on the other side (if you're fast enough: see step IV of my Syllabus Form, in *Advanced Longsword: Form and Function*), or default to yielding to the parry and entering with the pommel strike.

What should you do if your exchange fails?

As we have seen, the exchange can be countered in several ways. If your students are going to use this action confidently, they will need to be able to handle the situation if their exchange fails for some reason. So make sure they train counters to the counters. How would they deal with the yield-to-pommel-strike? With the exchange being parried on one side or the other?

These actions can be trained choreographically, as early in this process as you like. In fact I usually teach my students the complete four-step drill (attack, defence, counter to the defence, counter to the counter) before going really deep on adding a step before, or doing any of the steps competitively. At what stage would you include this step?

Applying the principle in other contexts

By this stage the students are more than ready to apply the exchange of thrusts in freeplay. But what about the general idea it represents: that as your opponent attacks, you counter them in the same tempo, with the same action?

At the end of the zogho largo section, on folio 27v, Fiore wrote:

> Here ends the wide play of the sword in two hands, that are plays together, which plays are: remedies, and counters from the forehand and the backhand side, and counterthrusts and countercuts of every type, with breaks, covers, strikes and binds, that all these things can be very easily understood.

Notice the counterthrust? As I see it, this refers to the exchange of thrusts. That Fiore also mentions (but as far as I can see does not show) countercuts, suggests that the lesson of this play can legitimately be applied to countering a cut with a cut. Liechtenauer practitioners will be jumping up and down squealing "*zornhau ort*!", and they are not wrong to do so.

At about the time that your students are comfortable enough with the basic drill that they are starting to play with the beginning of it, I would get them to apply the same idea by countering a *mandritto fendente* with a *mandritto fendente.*

The basic drill is easy to set up: both students begin in posta di donna destra, and as one attacks with a mandritto fendente, the other defends with the same blow, stepping out of the way. You can find the complete drill and explanations in of *From Medieval*

Manuscript to Modern Practice: the longsword techniques of Fiore dei Liberi, or see it on video here: https://guywindsor.net/2nddrillstretto

GREAT! Now you have the basic choreography of a basic action. What are you going to do with it?

This process of taking a basic action from the source and working with it until your students can actually apply it in practice is the real essence of what it means to be a historical martial arts instructor. I've said it before and I'll say it again: choreographical reproduction of the actions in The Book are a great starting point, but a terrible place to finish. What we're looking for is the ability to apply the actions in practice against a resistant opponent. This process is how we get from knowledge to skill.

CAPOFERRO'S PARRY RIPOSTE IN ONE TEMPO AS AN EXAMPLE OF SKILL DEVELOPMENT

The parry-riposte in one tempo is a foundational action from Capoferro's *Il Gran Simulacro* (plate 7) in which you defend against a thrust by counter-thrusting in the same tempo. Let's take a look at how we can create the basic drill from the text, then gradually train the students to apply the technique in more demanding circumstances. I should point out that you would not normally cover this whole process in a single session, unless you are working with quite advanced students from a different style (who are unfamiliar with this specific play). Most beginners will take a couple of years or more to get to the most advanced stages of this process.

Remember that *every* stage of this process should be trained according to the Rule of Cs (choreography, coaching, competition): once the choreography is understood, the students coach each other, and where appropriate compete to make their action work. This is why it takes so long! We are looking for skill, not just knowledge, and that takes time.

Also, the order is not precise— depending on the students, I may add the counter earlier, or add a step at the beginning earlier, and so on. This is just one way to do it.

I covered the basic action in detail in my *Rapier Workbook Part One: Beginners*, and I'll add the necessary details here in case you're unfamiliar with the action.

> THE PRESENT AND SUBSEQUENT FIGURES DEMONSTRATE DIVERSE MANNERS OF STRIKING ON THE OUTSIDE, ALWAYS Presupposing A Stringering On The Inside And A Disengage Of The Point By Your Adversary In Order To Strike
>
> By way of clarification of the following figures, I say that D having the figure marked C stringered on the inside, the same C disengages in order to give a thrust to the chest of figure D. D strikes them with a thrust in the left eye with a fixed foot or an increase of pace as the figure shows.
>
> But yet I say that if C had been a shrewd person, when he disengaged he would have disengaged by way of a feint, with his body somewhat held back, and D approaching confidently in order to attack C, C would have parried the enemy's sword to the outside with the false or the true edge, giving him a mandritto to the face or an imbroccata to the chest, and in such a conclusion would retire into a low quarta.

(TRANSLATION BY JHEREK SWANGER and William Wilson. Sorry about the shouty CAPS: they're in the original.)

Okay, so that's what Capoferro wrote. It's pretty damn confusing for most readers or listeners, so let me summarise the key points. Capoferro labels his figures according to their guard positions (A is prima, B is Seconda, C is terza, D is quarta): your opponent is in terza, and you stringer them in quarta; they disengage to strike you in the chest, and you parry-riposte in one tempo, through their left eye, lunging or not as needed.

So how do we teach the action without blinding anyone, and how do we develop the core skill that the action represents? Let's have a look.

The basic drill

Let's leave aside what your partner would have done if they had been a clever person (that's coming later) and focus on the illustrated action.

1. Your partner is in terza
2. You approach your partner, stringering their sword in quarta
3. Your partner disengages to strike in seconda
4. As they do so, catch their debole with your forte, turning your hand over (palm down). Aim your point at their left eye, and lunge. For safety's sake, your partner should leave out the lunge they were going to attack with.

If you've done everything right, it will look just like the plate, only (I hope) you will be training with clothes on. And masks. We call this 'step three of Plate 7'.

You can see the action on video here: https://guywindsor.net/blog/rbc011

The prerequisites:

To learn this play in its basic form, the students must know:

1. Basic safe training practices (control, use of masks, etc.)
2. The guards seconda, terza, and quarta
3. Stepping forwards and backwards
4. Stringering
5. The lunge
6. The disengage

7. The attack by disengage

THIS IS BASIC CHOREOGRAPHICAL STUFF, "so let's get the students coaching each other as soon as the choreography is reasonably solid, so long as the students are able to add a bit of intensity without adding significant risk. This will depend on their current level of training and available equipment.

I would usually start by having the one stringering use their closing of the line in seconda to train the one attacking with the disengage to execute the attack in measure, and in tempo, with decent structure behind it first. You can see this on video here:

https://guywindsor.net/blog/rbc306

THEN HAVE the one attacking by disengage train their partner to make the parry-riposte in one tempo better. You can see this on video here: https://guywindsor.net/blog/rbc309

SO WHAT'S the next step?

Given the way that we build up to teaching this action, students are already familiar with controlling the opponent's weapon, and the general principles of how to strike safely. So from here I would normally go directly to doing this action from the other side, which we see on plate 16. In Swanger and Wilson's translation, the text reads:

> THE PRESENT AND SUBSEQUENT FIGURES DEMONSTRATE DIVERSE WAYS OF STRIKING TO THE INSIDE ALWAYS PRESUPPOSING A Stringering On The Outside And A Disengaging Of The Point By Your Adversary In Order To Strike
>
> The following figures demonstrate diverse ways of striking on

> the inside, always presupposing on your side a stringering on the outside, and on that of your adversary, a disengage in order to strike you. D disengaging as above, C will strike him in quarta with a fixed foot, or with an increase of pace, in the throat or face. But if D had been an intelligent person, when he disengaged he would have disengaged with a beating of his enemy's sword with his edge, giving him a thrust to the face or a riverso to the arm of the figure designated as C, withdrawing into terza in ordinary pace.

The basic drill looks like this:

1. Your partner is in terza
2. Approach your partner, stringering their sword in seconda
3. Your partner disengages to strike in quarta
4. As they do so, catch their debole with your forte, turning your hand to quarta. Aim your point under their right ear. For safety's sake, your partner should leave out the lunge they were going to attack with.

Once the students have both of these basic drills, and have been coached to do both attacks by disengage and both parry-ripostes in one tempo to a basic standard, they can start playing with it. You could start by giving the one stringering a free choice of which side to enter. Or the one waiting to be stringered could arrange themselves so that one side of their sword is open to be stringered and the other isn't. This keeps things quite choreographical, but gets them thinking more deeply and moving better.

Preventing and countering:

The parry-riposte in one tempo is countered on plate 7 by a feint followed by a parry-riposte in two tempi, and it's prevented on plate 16 by doing a beat after the disengage.

I would teach these two options separately (see the *Complete*

Rapier Workbook pp 55 and 63) as choreographical drills first, then play with it. What happens if you do a beat when stringered on the inside? What happens if you feint when stringered on the outside?

'Who moves first?' At this stage we still have a completely static set-up. The defender is waiting in a static guard, the attacker attacks from a static guard. This is highly unnatural, so let's play with it by getting the defender to move first. Generally speaking, it's best to vary one side of the drill at a time. You could use Hunt the Debole with or without footwork to create a less static beginning to the drill, while keeping it quite restricted. The roles should be agreed in advance at this stage, and the attack by disengage should only happen if the one doing it thinks they have a reasonable chance to strike.

Once this is comfortable, you could have both students starting out of measure, and approaching each other, trying to stringer or counter-stringer.

The parry-riposte in one tempo in other contexts: this action should work whenever your opponent attacks by disengage. So how can you persuade them to do so?

And, can it work when the opponent's attack is not preceded by a disengage?

Does the entry with a thrust closing the line against a downwards blow, as shown on Plate 10 (see the Complete Rapier Workbook p. 93), count as a parry-riposte in one tempo? If not, why not?

By this stage the students are more than ready to be applying the parry-riposte in one tempo in freeplay.

This process of taking a basic action from the source and working with it until your students can actually apply it in practice is the real essence of what it means to be a historical martial arts instructor. I've said it before and I'll say it again: choreographical reproduction of the actions in The Book are a great starting point, but a terrible place to finish. What we're looking for is the ability to apply the actions in practice against a resistant opponent. This process is how we get from knowledge to skill.

PREPARING YOUR STUDENTS FOR FREEPLAY

We have systematically added complexity to our basic choreographical drills, by adding steps at the beginning, at the end, adding degrees of freedom, and training everything choreographically, as a coaching exercise, and competitively. What we need now then is a drill that allows either person to attack or defend, with any action, and the play to continue until a technique is successfully concluded. We call it freeplay!

It is relatively easy to set up a freeplay environment that is reasonably safe. I have seen many groups and schools that have nice set drills, and freeplay quite a bit, but there is no real relationship between the two kinds of training. The things done in freeplay bear scant resemblance to the actions in the drills. The point of this section is to show you how to build a bridge between set drills and freeplay. This is especially important for historical swordsmanship, as the manuals tend to show short, simple sequences (an attack and a defence, usually) which are easy to turn into drills, but very hard to pull off in friendly freeplay.

Freeplay of some kind is a key component of most martial arts. How you should prepare for it depends on what your freeplay is supposed to accomplish, and where freeplay-like activities fit into your system. Schools that emphasise winning tournaments tend to introduce it very early, using heavily modified weapon simulators and lots of protection (my earliest formal weapons training was sport fencing; I seem to remember that we did freeplay at the end of the first class); schools that emphasise other things, such as historical accuracy, tend to modify the weapons less, use less protection, and so naturally introduce it much later. The trick then is to build a bridge between the set drills based on techniques from your historical source, and competitive freeplay.

Let's start easy; if getting beginners to freeplay quickly is your goal, then all you have to do is have:

1. Safer weapons (eg nylon longswords, or sport-fencing foils, or similar) and adequate protection
2. Rules, such as a list of what is allowed and what is not (e.g. no throws, kicks, chokes, or whatever)
3. Supervision: make sure that everybody is wearing the right protection and follows the rules.

As they develop their skills, you might graduate them to more realistic weapons, or less protection, or allow a wider variety of techniques. Some students will be put off if the freeplay appears too unstructured, so be ready to introduce beginners gently, such as by letting a senior student who can be relied on to go easy on them at first be their first opponent.

As the instructor it is up to you to determine the rules of engagement. There are two parts to the rules: the code of conduct determining how freeplay should be set up, and the actual scoring ruleset that they will fence under. The former deals with things like equipment, levels of force, permitted techniques etc.; the latter with what constitutes a scoring action. To my mind, the code of conduct should stay the same at all times, but you should vary the ruleset as necessary to develop whatever skills you are trying to impart. So for instance the code of conduct determines that the students must be wearing adequate hand protection, while the ruleset states whether hand hits score points.

The rules can be adapted further to develop specific aspects of technique: for instance, you may not allow any close quarters work at all, or you may restrict allowable hits to one small target.

Make sure that all participants have a very clear understanding of both the code and the rules before they face off.

Freeplay code of conduct

Here is my normal code of conduct for freeplay.

Participants must:

1. Agree on a mutually acceptable level of safety.

2. Wear at least the minimum amount of safety gear commensurate with rule 1.

3. Confine allowable technique to those within the limits of your equipment.

4. Confine allowable technique to the technical ability of the least trained combatant.

5. Appoint either an experienced student or one of the combatants to preside over the bout.

6. Agree on allowable targets.

7. Agree on what constitutes a hit.

8. Agree on priority in the event of simultaneous hits. Usually it is better to allow a fatal blow before a minor wound, but simultaneous hits should be avoided whenever possible.

9. Agree on the duration of the bout either in terms of hits, such as first to five, or in real time.

10. Acknowledge all hits against yourself. This can be done by raising an arm, or by stopping the bout with a salute, or by calling "Halt!" and telling your opponent where and how you think they hit you.

11. Maintain self-command at all times.

. . .

TAKE a moment to consider what code you want your students to fence under. Write them down and discuss them with your colleagues and students.

Then write up at least two scoring rulesets, and think about what incentives they create. If a throw scores three points and a hit to the hands scores one, what kind of fencing do you think your students will exhibit? It's important for you to have a clear idea of what actions you want to reward, and what behaviour you want to discourage.

There are several ways to set up freeplay in the salle, depending on your goals and the number of available participants. Common setups require 2, 3, 5, or 7 participants. The simplest is two fencers get together, agree on the rules, and fence, governing themselves. But it can be useful to have a third person there to evaluate what happened and assign points. This ups the formality a bit, and provides the referee with the opportunity to work on their fencing memory and ability to understand what they just saw.

Most HMA tournaments have bouts performed in a circular area, with a ring director and two judges. Each fencer has a red or a blue armband, and each judge has two flags, red and blue, that they use to indicate blows struck. If you plan on going to this kind of tournament you should certainly try to set up the same circumstances in the salle. It is also useful for the judges and the ring directors to get some practice.

The classical fencing setup is designed to work on a rectangular fencing strip (the piste), and has two judges per fencer. The ones standing behind you watch your opponent's target area for any hits you may land, and ignore everything coming towards you. Your opponent's judges do the same for them, and the director (or president) runs the bout, and polls the judges for what they saw.

All of these modes have their pros and cons. As a teacher, you should be able to fulfil any of the roles (fencer, judge, director), and so should make sure to get some practice in at all of them from time to time.

So that's how to set up freeplay: how do we use it as a training tool? That's next…

USING FREEPLAY IN TRAINING

What is freeplay good for?

That may seem like a silly question. To most sword people, it's why they do swords. Freeplay is what we do, right?

Well, yes and no, depending on your goals. Learning to fence by just doing freeplay is like learning to box by just boxing. Literally no high-level boxer would consider that approach— there's conditioning, footwork drills, bag work, speedball work, working with your coach, etc etc.

There is nothing wrong with a student showing up to freeplay sessions, fencing their friends, and going home again. But if they get frustrated with their progress, as they probably will, it's your job as the teacher to know how to use freeplay as a training tool.

Firstly, freeplay is an excellent diagnostic tool for your fencing technique, and a good opponent will highlight your weaknesses for you clearly and unambiguously. It is less effective as a diagnostic tool for matters of historical interpretation, unless your equipment and ruleset are accurate reproductions of the context for which your historical system was developed.

I will often open an advanced class with some freeplay to help the students figure out what they should be working on. The options below can all be done with or without a director and/or judges. Adjust the level of protective gear based on the level of intensity. Safety first, always.

1. Slow-motion freeplay, in which if you have to speed up to defend yourself, that counts as a hit against you.

2. Fence to one hit, then recreate the hit, identify the problem, drill the solution, and play again.

3. Fence to five or more hits with the same partner, then recreate the most common problem and fix it.

4. Fence to five hits or so with several partners, looking for a pattern in how you are getting hit. It may be that you are only vulnerable to a particular fencer's way of throwing a feint, for instance.

5. Fence with artificial restrictions, such as A can only strike with a cut to the head. B can do what they like. Or A cannot initiate the attack, they have to wait for B. These restrictions should not be arbitrary— you choose them to allow the fencers to highlight or work on specific weaknesses.

6. Playing with the artificial restrictions idea, see what happens when the fencers aren't aware of the restrictions imposed on the other, or are aware. I often use a deck of Audatia cards to randomly assign guards, blows, or stretto plays to the fencers. (Audatia is a card game teaching the structure and theory of Fiore's longsword plays that I developed and published: see audatiagame.com.)

7. Stand your ground: one fencer waits, and every other member of the class lines up to attack them one at a time. These attacks can be free, or restricted. The defender may be working on not giving ground, or a specific counter, or just dealing with a lot of variety in not much time. Each pass can be fought to a conclu-

sion, or to a breaking off, or the attacker can be restricted to just the one action.

8. Cover your ground: the same set-up as stand your ground, but the defender can initiate the action. The fencers start at opposite ends of the salle and move towards each other. When the pass is concluded, the next person in line begins their approach. Decide how much time, if any, the defender gets between passes, depending on your training goals.

Freeplay is just another drill, that has a certain set of degrees of freedom, and so it can be used and adapted like any other drill. There is no limit to the number of possible variations. As the teacher, it's your job to get the students using whatever version of freeplay suits their training goals the best.

Next, let's have a look at troubleshooting. What do you do when your student is getting hit?

TROUBLESHOOTING

Your students will encounter problems all the time, especially if they are training at the optimal rate of failure. In fact, they should be deliberately seeking out areas of weakness by running regular diagnostic drills.

A diagnostic drill is any activity that is done for the purposes of showing you what to train next. For instance, a basic movement exercises at the beginning of the warm-up tells you what bits of your body need limbering up. Repeating it after you have warmed up will tell you how effective your warm-up was. Freeplay is often used as a diagnostic drill: any time you get hit, there must have been something you did that allowed the hit to land. Diagnostic drills can be used to expose areas of strength, and also gaps in your knowledge, and areas where you are lacking in skill.

When a diagnostic drill exposes an issue, whatever that issue is the overall process for working on it is the same. It goes like this:

1. Recreate the problem
2. Determine whether it is tactical or technical
3. Choose whether you want to prevent it or counter it, and work out the solution choreographically

4. Use the multipliers to train the solution at the optimal rate of failure

5. Run the diagnostic again.

Recreate the problem

If the problem is vague, re-run the diagnostic (or recreate the original conditions), and let it occur a few times, to establish exactly what it is. If you can't recreate the problem, you can't solve it.

For instance, in freeplay, your student gets hit on the hands a lot.

Is it when they are attacking or defending? Or in a neutral situation? When they are moving from the right and the left, or just one side? Against opponents of a certain type, or one individual, or just generally? Does the strike come from above, below, or both? And so on.

The more detail the better, such as: "I get hit on the hands when recovering from a failed attack, if my opponent is on my outside line, and usually from above. It doesn't happen during my attack, or on my inside line."

Is the problem technical or tactical?

This problem could be occurring because of the student's mechanics as they withdraw leaving an uncoverable opening (technical: doing the right thing not well enough), or because they are not parrying the strike (tactical: they are doing the wrong thing by omitting the parry). This will determine how you set up the solution: either working on their sword handling mechanics, or adding a parry.

. . .

Prevent or counter?

You can prevent the problem by training the student to avoid the situation in which it occurs. For instance, they could withdraw differently, so that their hands are not exposed. Or they can deliberately create the opening, to draw their opponent's action onto the student's prepared counter. Both of these options work, and which you choose will depend on the exact situation and the student's goals. It should be quite straightforward to set up a drill in which the student is able to prevent or counter the strike to the hands. You can of course work on both, but do so separately. If the action is prevented, it can't be countered.

Train at the optimal rate of failure

Using the multipliers (add a step, degrees of freedom, etc.) creates a context in which the student's partner can generate the optimal rate of failure for them (i.e. coach them). In an individual lesson, that partner is you, of course.

Keep building up the complexity and intensity until it matches or surpasses the context in which the problem occurred naturally. This may take many sessions, over weeks or months, or it might get solved in five minutes. It depends entirely on the problem being solved and the skill levels of the coach and the student.

Run the diagnostic again

When you think the problem is probably solved, run the diagnostic again. There are three possible outcomes:

1. The problem is solved (or is at least not the worst problem shown up by the diagnostic). Yay! Find a new problem.

2. The problem is the same or worse. Your training method is not working, so you need to re-assess your approach. Were you actually working on the exact problem? Were you really gener-

ating the optimal rate of failure? This situation is actually quite rare, with students who are familiar with this method.

3. The problem is better but still needs work. So continue with your current approach, and increase the complexity and/or intensity to get the optimal rate of failure.

There is a snazzy flowchart of this process on the resources page for this book, at guywindsor.net/howtoteachresources. Refer to it often, it's the fundamental pattern of skill development.

THIS APPROACH IS VERY SIMPLE, but as with so many simple things, it's not easy. It requires discipline and focus, or very quickly it will deteriorate into mindless repetition or general bish-bash-bosh. It's your job as the teacher to create the environment in which the disciplined approach is simply expected, and natural. Make sure you do incorporate some time in training for blowing off steam though: it will refresh your students for the next round of deliberate practice.

So far we have covered all the basic teaching skills. But teaching is much easier if you have a clear, well structured, syllabus to follow. So how do we create one? That's next...

PART VI
CREATING A SYLLABUS

SYLLABUS DESIGN

As a teacher it is up to you to make sure that the students have a syllabus to follow. If you are working within an established school you may not have any say in the structure and content of the syllabus itself, but even so you should understand how to use the syllabus for the benefit of the students. Ideally though you will be able to adjust the syllabus based on your observations of how the students develop while working through it.

The hallmarks of a well-designed syllabus are:

1. A clear goal. Is the syllabus intended to create a good fencer in one style, an all-round martial artist, a competent researcher, or something else?

2. Every action in the higher levels have been prepared for in the lower levels.

3. Students can reliably progress through the levels to reach their goals. If students are getting stuck at a particular point, then the syllabus is probably lacking in some material.

4. There is scope for more than one route through the material, allowing students to follow their interests at least up to a point.

. . .

THE FOUNDATION of your syllabus is a set of between three and seven drills that will form literally the foundation or basic training for your students. The idea is that once they know those three to seven drills, they have a solid handle on the fundamental techniques, tactics, and ideas behind the system.

SO HOW DO we create drills?

Most martial arts have a foundation of a few core drills. When I build a syllabus, I like to create a single cornerstone drill, from which all the others can be developed. To do this, you must first know what drills are for, and how they are constructed. The principles of creating drills are:

1. Put first things first
2. Every drill should teach one thing
3. Distinguish between breadth and depth
4. Distinguish between tactical and technical.

Let's take these one at a time.

1. Put first things first. This is important because in every drill there's a certain amount of assumed knowledge. When you're creating your drills, you have to start with the assumed knowledge being zero. If your drill has an attack and a defence in it, you must make sure that the attack is taught first, possibly in a separate drill. So put first things first and make sure that the drill doesn't depend on any knowledge that the students do not yet have.

2. Every drill should teach one thing. There is a primary purpose to every drill you create. Of course, there may be many secondary purposes and the drill can be practiced for all sorts purposes, but in its essence the drill should have one primary purpose. For

instance, it might represent a specific play from a specific treatise in a trainable and accessible way, or it might develop the ability to deceive with feints. Those are two completely separate types of drills. The classic rookie mistake when creating drills is to try and cram too much stuff in. If your drill successfully teaches one thing, it is a good drill. If it successfully teaches two things at once, it's an impossible drill.

3. Distinguish between breadth and depth. Breadth is knowing many things. A drill that has you go through all nine masters of the dagger from *Il Fior di Battaglia* teaches breadth. Depth is being able to do those things under pressure, such as taking one of those masters and using his defence against resistant opponents. In their basic form, the drills you create will emphasize either breadth or depth. These are not entirely mutually exclusive, but you should be clear at the outset whether your drill is intended to teach a series of things to expand the student's knowledge, or to teach the ability to do a particular thing better than they could do it before.

4. Distinguish between technical and tactical. A technical drill tells you how to do something. A tactical drill tells you when to do it and why. These are fundamentally different problems. If for example I got hit in the head because I didn't know that I should have parried, I'd need a tactical drill to teach me that in this circumstance the parry is the correct response. If I parried but my parry failed because it wasn't good enough, then I need a technical drill to teach me how to parry better. In every drill that you create, you should distinguish between technical and tactical and in their basic form, every drill should be either a technical drill or a tactical drill. At the basic level of the syllabus, every drill is a technical drill

because your students don't yet know the techniques on which the system is built.

Types of drill

Drills can be solo or done in pairs, and sometimes in multiple opponent situations.

Every solo drill at this stage is a technical drill. Every pair drill can be either technical or tactical. So we must distinguish between drills which are intended to be trained alone, and drills which are intended to be trained in pairs. In general, a handling drill which makes you flip the sword around in all sorts of funny ways is a technical drill, but has no tactical application and so shouldn't be done with a partner. The drills you're going to come up with will emphasize either technique, tactics, or attributes.

Technical drills are the base of most martial arts systems. Your syllabus will be founded on technical drills that teach the student the fundamental actions of the system.

Tactical drills teach you when you should do what. Any drill that includes choice is a tactical drill.

Attribute **training** develops attributes like strength, speed, timing, weapons handling, judgement of measure, or tactical awareness. A push-up is an attribute training drill; a footwork line drill is an attribute training drill too.

. . .

LET'S take a straight punch as an example. Weight training that develops arm strength and improves your punch is attribute training. Technical practice, such as on the heavy bag, improves your punching technique (something that bench presses do not do). Training on the striking mitts with a coach teaching you when to use your straight punch is tactical training.

AT THE MORE ADVANCED LEVEL, drills do tend to work on more than one of these factors. For example, if your technical drill is being trained hard and fast for the purpose of developing the attribute of speed, we can call it an advanced technical drill.

The drill in which you train tactics, technique, and attributes, all at once is freeplay. As you would expect, anything that does more than one thing at a time tends to be not terribly efficient at doing any one of those things, but in a fight, you must be able to apply your solid technique with speed and strength, at the right time. It is necessary that you have the opportunity to practice all of these things together at least at some point.

When you are creating a drill, you need to think to yourself where would it fit in this model. Is it:

- a purely tactical drill that relies on a certain assumed technical knowledge?
- a purely attribute drill which requires no knowledge or technique?
- a technical drill which can be done slowly and calmly and without any sense of tactics at all while the students are learning the basic choreography?

The Bullshit Theory of Drill Design

Every drill has a dollop of bullshit built in. It has to. The important thing is that you should know what that dollop is. The real thing is the only bullshit-free scenario in martial arts. If you're an MMA fighter, that's the ring on fight night. If you're a soldier, that's being in the presence of the enemy. And if you are a swordfighter, that is someone trying to take your head off with a blade. But the real thing must be prepared for, so we have drills, exercises and training. Problems only arise when we mistake one scenario (a training drill) for another (the real thing). To properly understand any drill, you must have a clear idea of exactly how it deviates from reality. I call this spotting the bullshit.

Let us take a simple example, a drill that is usually included in day one of our Fiore beginners' course: the basic execution of Fiore's first play of the dagger. This technique is a disarm, done against the common overhand blow.

In its basic set-up, the drill goes like this:

Both players start left foot forwards, hands down, in a proper guard position. This is very artificial, and is intended only to create a consistent starting point for beginners.

1. Attacker and defender both in porta di ferro, left foot forwards.
2. Attacker passes to strike with a fendente. Aim it at the mask!
3. Defender intercepts attacker's wrist with his left hand and
4. Turns it to the left, creating a leverage disarm with the dagger against the back of his wrist.
5. Defender collects dagger and strikes

THERE IS nothing wrong with this, as a starting point. But it has at least the following dollops of bullshit in it:

1. The attacker is not trying to kill you.
2. The weapon is not sharp.
3. The roles are pre-set, attacker and defender.
4. You can't really run away or call the cops.
5. You have to wait for the attack.

6. You are wearing protective gear, that will allow the attacker to make contact, but would not work against a real dagger (we tried this with a mask on a dummy: the mask failed against all medieval weaponry).

7. The line of the attack is pre-selected.

8. Your defence is pre-selected.

9. The attacker is not allowed to counter or continue.

10. The attack is done with little force.

11. The attack is done slowly.

I am sure that you can think of other dollops, but 11 is enough to be going on with. So, how do we deal with this? How can we eliminate the bullshit without killing students?

To start with, number one cannot be trained outside of the real scenario. Don't even try. It is this one element that really makes the difference between those that have done it for real and those that haven't. (I haven't and don't intend to.) Regarding combat sports, you haven't done it till you've been in the ring or competed in a serious tournament. Fortunately, those are much more survivable environments, so anybody who trains seriously enough can get there and do that art 'for real'. This is one of the big attractions of combat sports I think: the real environment is available. I will never forget my first fencing competition. It was an eye-opener, to say the least!

So, if my drill above is so full of bullshit, why do we do it?

It does:

1. Teach core mechanical principles, such as grounding, finding lines of weakness, etc.

2. Teach core tactical principles, such as control the weapon before you strike; timing, and control of distance.

3. Given the source of our art, it gives beginners a chance to reconstruct a technique from the book.

It is a perfectly good starting point. Just as a child learning to read sounding out the individual letters and creating the words is not really reading yet, we don't say that they should just recognise the words straight away. This level of practice is a necessary step on the way to expertise.

But be aware that this drill does NOT:

1. Teach a survival skill.
2. Teach situational awareness.
3. Teach decision making or judgement.
4. Teach the ability to execute the action under pressure.

But given our list of eleven dollops of bullshit, we can map a route through training to systematically eliminate each of them in turn (except for the first). By applying the 'who moves first' multiplier, for instance, we can eliminate point 5 on our list of dollops, so the defender is not required to wait, but can enter or move away, gaining some control. By allowing degrees of freedom for one or other student, we can eliminate 7, 8 and/or 9. By applying the Rule of Cs you can increase the intensity in a systematic way, so eliminating 10 and 11.

It is very important to not eliminate all the bullshit all at once. Especially when eliminating no. 2 by practising with sharps, you should absolutely keep all sorts of other bullshit present to avoid serious injury.

So, by carefully considering all the ways in which a set drill is not a real fight, you can design variations to the basic version to systematically clean up some of the bullshit. You will need lots of different drills, each with a different bullshit profile, to make sure that you are training in all of the attributes of the 'real' technique.

Now that we have got that out of the way, the first step in creating your syllabus is to design what I call the 'cornerstone drill'.

CREATE THE CORNERSTONE

My cornerstone drills (I have one for every sword style I teach) are always a four step drill in which everything that is vital to the system is represented in some way. The four steps are usually an attack countered by a defence which is countered by a counter to the defence which is countered by a counter to the counter to the defence.

The four steps:

1. Attack
2. Defence
3. Counter to the defence
4. Counter to the counter.

THE CRITICAL THING about the cornerstone drill is it must be representative of the system as a whole. If there are all sorts of sneaky little techniques which occur once in the system in a very specific context, they may be interesting and important, but you'll get onto those later. Your cornerstone drill should be primarily technical. To begin with it will be trained slowly and carefully, not developing any particular attributes and, while it represents a set of tactical preferences, it is not a tactical drill because it doesn't include options at this stage.

With your cornerstone, you want something that represents as closely as possible the fundamental tactical and technical preferences of the system that you are trying to represent. This is quite a tall order and there will be lots of little side quests as you progress through creating your cornerstone drill, and if it makes you feel any better, the cornerstone drill that is the foundation of my Fiore syllabus in my school took, I think, 11 years to get to its current and hopefully final incarnation. So don't worry if you don't get it absolutely perfect first time, you're in good company. As long as you have a clear idea of what you're trying to accomplish, you should find getting there a lot quicker than the 11 years it seemed to take me.

THERE ARE six steps to creating and teaching your cornerstone drill.

1. A solo technical drill where you start out with choosing an attack that is commonly used in your system
2. Create the drill that is the defence against that specific attack
3. Take that defence out and create a drill in which you practice it solo
4. Put them back together and explain the tactics behind it. This gives you an idea of how drills in general are constructed
5. Add the attacker's counter to the defence and explain the tactics behind it
6. Add the defender's counter to the attacker's counter to the defence.

. . .

There are therefore six steps overall to create a four step drill. The two extra steps are a solo practice of step 1 (the attack), and solo practice of the second step of the drill (the defence).

Step 1 of the drill: the attack

Begin with one or two basic actions from your source, such as an *oberhau,* a kick, a *mandritto fendente* or a lunge in *quarta* and recover. Then create a standardised way in which to practice it. You need a standard starting position which is followed by the movement and then followed by however you recover from it.

It could be for instance: I start in posta di donna, I cut *mandritto fendente* with a pass, I end in *dente di zengiaro,* and I pass back. Or: I stand in on guard in *terza,* I extend in *quarta,* I lunge and I recover.

Then you need to explain (at least to yourself, but ideally write it down with as much detail as possible) why you've chosen each part of that drill. So why *posta di donna*? Why *quarta*?

Then identify any prerequisite knowledge and suddenly you'll realize that well, okay, your students don't know posta di donna yet, or they don't know how to hold a sword properly, or, if your drill includes ninja assassin techniques, they don't know their backflips yet (it is a truth universally acknowledged that you've got to be able to do backflips to be a ninja assassin). Your first side-quest on the way to creating the cornerstone drill will be to note down that these elements will have to be trained either in their own separate drill or as part of the drill that you are trying to create. There is already all sorts of room for adding breadth, so on your second side-quest you could repeat this exercise for every single common strike in the system. Mandritto fendente, roverso fendente, mandritto sottano, roverso sottano, different lunges and passes and so forth. You'll notice if you have a look in my syllabus for the longsword, we have the Cutting Drill and the Syllabus Form which do all that. We also have it in the rapier footwork form, which contains all of the footwork actions that are commonly used in Capoferro's system.

Don't go off on these side-quests just yet because we're still working on the cornerstone drill. Just note that you'll need to expand in these directions later.

STEP TWO OF THE DRILL: the defence

Choose a counter to the action that you've just trained, ideally directly from the source. For example, against a mandritto fendente, you could parry from tutta porta di ferro, or, against the lunge in quarta, you could counterattack also in quarta. (I don't know how ninja assassins defend against a back-flip.) Then set up the drill so that you know what everyone is doing and why. You should notice at this stage that most of the plays we find in most of the sources are usually a simple defence against a simple attack.

However, they are often preceded by implied or stated actions. Let's take plate seven from Capoferro for example. The text (in William Wilson's and Jherek Swanger's translation) reads:

> By way of clarification of the following figures, I say that D having the figure marked C stringered on the inside, the same C disengages in order to give a thrust to the chest of figure D. D strikes him with a thrust in the left eye with a fixed foot or an increase of pace as the figure shows.
>
> But yet I say that if C had been a shrewd person, when he disengaged he would have disengaged by way of a feint, with his body somewhat held back, and D approaching confidently in order to attack C, C would have parried the enemy's sword to the outside with the false or the true edge, giving him a mandritto to the face or an imbroccata to the chest, and in such a conclusion

would retire into a low quarta.

The action begins with your opponent standing on guard in terza, and you approach them in quarta. If they did nothing, you would just hit them. However, as you approach them in quarta, they disengage, find your sword, and stab you through the chest in seconda. That is the attack that is stated in the text and shown in the picture being done by the figure on the left. But as you approach them, you stringer them in quarta and they disengage to strike in seconda, you parry and strike in a single motion, stabbing them through the left eye in seconda. That is the actual play that the plate shows. That presupposes that you know how to stringere in quarta and that your opponent knows how to attack by disengage. The cornerstone drill that we use for our rapier training is this one from plate seven, but it must be preceded by exercises on how to stringere, and exercises on how to attack by disengage because without those, there is no way to set up the situation that occurs on plate seven.

IN MOST CIRCUMSTANCES it's a good idea to extract the defender's part of the drill and practice it solo so you have a nice start, middle, and end. For example, if I'm doing a parry from tutta porta di ferro against a mandritto fendente coming from posta di donna, you should practice the parry movement by itself, particularly if this is in a very basic class. Being able to do the movement correctly makes doing the action a lot easier but having somebody actually trying to hit you in the head while you're trying to do your movement makes everything more complicated. It's a good idea, particularly at the basic level, to extract the defender's action and practice it as a movement in its own right.

Explain to yourself or to the students what exactly is going on, the tactical rationale for making the defence the way you're doing it. It's not enough to just repeat it slavishly from the book. It's not a bad start but it's not sufficient. You need to understand why every action is as it is, and for that you are going to need to have a pretty solid idea as to why this particular defence should be done in this particular context. If you're new to this, don't worry. This level of information or level of expertise will develop over time.

Step 3 of the drill: **the attacker's counter**

Having put the drill back together, then add the next step, which is the attacker's counter to the defence. Ideally source it from the book. For instance, in the plate seven example above, Capoferro is kind enough to state that if C had been a clever person, he would have disengaged by way of a feint and, D coming to strike, C would parry and riposte. That's ideal. Likewise, Fiore gives us a counter which is good "against all the plays that come before it" which is to yield and pommel strike. We use that for step three of our First Drill. (You can find the play on f.44v of the Getty ms.)

Now explain the tactics behind the attacker's continuation.

If your book doesn't have a specific counter to that defence in the context of that defence being made, in other words as an actual continuation of that defence, you're going to have to find it from somewhere else in the book. If your book doesn't have attacker's continuations against defences, then we have to wonder whether that book is actually fit for purpose, because you do need to have a solid grasp of all the parts of fencing and ideally you need to get those from a historical source before you end up making stuff up. You are going to need to be able to fence past the first defence.

Step four of the drill: **the defender's counter to the counter**

Add the defender's counter to the attacker's counter to the

defence. Again, ideally sourced from the book. The logic behind this is the same as for the previous step and again, you need to be able to explain why you're doing it this way. At this level, simply saying "it says to do this in the book" is actually sufficient because this is all about historical authenticity. If you don't understand the why of it yet but the book tells you to do it, just do it. But before you start teaching this to some unsuspecting beginner students it's a good idea if you have at least a solid working theory of why it would be this way.

Building on the Cornerstone Drill

Congratulations, you now have one solid four step drill: attack, defence, counter to the defence, counter to the counter. That is sufficient for your cornerstone drill. However, you'll have noticed that at every stage there are all sorts of possibilities for variations. You could choose a different attack, or it could be a different defence against the same attack, or it could be a different counter to the same defence against the same attack, and so on. Once you have your cornerstone drill, and you've worked through a few options and come up with something you're really happy with, it will give you the basic structure of the system and ideally every further drill that you create can be expressed as a variation on this basic drill.

For example, if we take the cornerstone drill for my Fiore syllabus for the longsword, First drill, we have:

1. *Mandritto fendente* from *posta di donna*
2. Parry from *tutta porta di ferro* and strike
3. Yield to the parry and pommel strike
4. Cover against the pommel strike and do your own pommel strike.

In our Second drill, the attack is the same but the defence is from a different guard, dente di zenghiaro on the left. The third basic drill is the exchange of thrust, in which the attack is a thrust. Indeed, all of our longsword technical drills can be expressed as variations on First Drill.

Similarly, in our rapier syllabus our cornerstone drill is plate seven, and the second foundational drill is plate 16 in which you stringer on the outside, which is countered by an attack by disengage. You could think of it as 'plate seven on the other side'.

By building your syllabus on a cornerstone drill, all the other drills can be expressed as variations on it, and this makes the whole syllabus much easier to remember and much easier for the students to absorb as a complete system, rather than as a set of isolated techniques.

So now you have your cornerstone drill, let's have a look at building it out into a syllabus. That's next…

BUILDING UP THE SYLLABUS

The golden rule of syllabus design is this: you must only teach them a drill for which they already have the necessary components. Every next step in the syllabus must be prepared for by the previous steps. If a new drill introduces, for example, a new blow, they have to be taught that blow first so when they see the drill, they already know its components.

In a syllabus made up of three levels, everything they did in level one prepares them for level two and the new material in level two will prepare them for level three. When you created the cornerstone drill in the previous part, you established what you feel is the fundamental technique, the fundamental idea of the system, so you've already done a lot of the preparation work for creating this foundation. We're going to take that same process, those same ideas and apply them in a slightly broader way.

Firstly, you have to identify the key plays. You've probably already done this as part of the winnowing out process of choosing your cornerstone drill but this is just a reminder to identify the key plays. You should look for plays that are repeated or patterns that are repeated within the source that you're working with and your key plays will also solve common problems. For example, if in your system a thrust to the face is very common, your foundational plays must address it. If though, for example, a cut to the ankle occurs once in a 400-page book, it's probably not going to appear in your foundation. You might include it in the full syllabus but you won't put it into the foundation. So, the foundation is, if you like, the 80/20 principle at work where 20% of actions apply to 80% of the context.

Let's take a concrete example. In my foundational syllabus for the longsword, we have four drills around which everything else is built.

1. First drill deals with mandritto fendente (a forehand descending blow coming to your left shoulder), which is parried from the right.
2. Second drill has the same attack, but it's parried from the left.
3. Third drill is the "exchange of thrusts", defending from your right side against a thrust coming from your opponent's right side.
4. Fourth drill is the "breaking of the thrust", defending from your right side against a thrust coming for your opponent's left side.

What this gives you is an attack with a cut, an attack with a thrust, attacks from both the right and the left, and defences against a cut and a thrust from the right and the left. This is a broad and expandable set of material, with each of these plays sourced directly from Fiore's manuscript. This means they fit together quite nicely as a coherent whole and when the student has that and all the necessary training to be able to do those drills, then they have the basic breadth required to expand outwards into dealing with attacks from below and attacks from above and so on. A well-built foundation is easily expanded upon.

. . .

How many drills should the foundation have?

I prefer between three and seven. Less than three is usually not enough to cover the fundamentals, and more than seven are difficult to hold in memory at once. Ideally, your foundational syllabus, the core drills that you're going to build everything around, can be held relatively easily in memory. Most people's working memory is limited to between five and nine individual items, and that's pretty much hardwired. So, seven is on the high side, most people should be able to manage five, three and you're maybe starting to lose some of the opportunity to make your syllabus a bit broader. The best way to find the exact number is to see where the material takes you. If there seems to be four basic ideas, have four drills.

One of my students on the Recreate Historical Swordsmanship from Historical Sources course is creating a syllabus for the I.33 sword and buckler manual. It says in the very beginning of the manuscript that there are seven wards or guards, of which three "take the fore". In other words, three are the most important. So he decided to make three drills the foundation of his syllabus.

Having established what your foundational drills are, you need to figure out what a student needs to know before they can be taught those drills. This may include sword handling exercises, footwork exercises, even fitness training.

The foundation should be enough material that it would normally take about four to six months to cover it all with a beginner who is training about twice a week for an hour and a half a time. Obviously, you might be able to run an experienced swordsman through the whole thing in 20 minutes.

It's a good idea at this stage when you're putting together your foundational material to design the basic components of a beginners course of six to ten classes. This will force you to organize and prioritize your material. Your cornerstone drill will be there, and its prerequisites too, but see what else of your foundation will fit in. In that process of trimming your four to six months of material down to a six to ten classes section, it'll give you a way of prioritizing the material, a way of thinking about it that will be very useful.

Creating a syllabus is a monumental task, and as with any such challenge, the best approach is to break it down into manageable chunks. You already have your cornerstone drill, and your foundation. The next step is to expand the foundation, using two approaches, which we might label 'Theory' and 'Practice'.

Theory

First, you need to work out a complete interpretation for your primary source. This may take a very long time, and you should go at it section by section. Pick a section and work through it, writing down each and every play or technique as a separate drill. You need to know who is doing what at every stage of the action, and unless the book specifically states otherwise, both combatants should be doing something that might work. Keep going with this until you have worked through every play in every section, and have your working interpretation of every play written down. This will take a long time, but it's fun, fascinating, and useful, so there's no rush.

As you go through the book, note which techniques come up repeatedly, and what appear to be solutions to highly specific situations. Both of these categories need to be incorporated in your syllabus, with the most common actions at the most basic level. Depending on how the plays are written out in the book, you may need to add actions to them to create workable drills; very often, fencing manuals have 'you're in this situation, do this' instruction, without ever telling you what you did to get into that situation. You need to figure that out.

. . .

Practice

No book is perfectly comprehensive. It is simply impossible to write down every possible variation, because the art is infinitely complex. There are more possible combinations of sword actions than there are atoms in the universe, because every action can be countered, so there is, in theory, no end to the permutations you might come up with. This is not useful. So instead of trying to work out every possible variation, you need a set of multipliers, with which you can develop variations on your foundational drills, which will often magically lead you into plays from the book. I go over these multipliers in detail in the section on Freeplay Preparation, so will just recap them briefly here. The multipliers I use are:

- Who moves first? You can start the drill with both players standing still in guard (this is the usual set-up for beginners to start with), or you can change who attacks, or the defender can draw the attack by some prior movement or invitation.
- Add a step: you can add a counter to the end of any drill, or you can add a preparation or some other action at the beginning.
- Degrees of freedom: at any stage in any drill, a set of decisions have been made. Systematically allowing a different choice to be made by one player, on the fly, introduces an element of unpredictability for the other player.
- The Rule of Cs: this is not strictly a multiplier, but it gives you the three main attitudes with which every drill should be practised. Co-operate, Coach, and Compete.

These multipliers (or any you develop yourself) should be incorporated into the syllabus itself, as should any specific drills they create that you find solve a common problem for your students.

Now all that remains is to run cohorts of students through it, and see what happens. Are they getting stuck somewhere? Then the rungs of the ladder are too far apart at that point. Are they exhibiting common errors? Then the training needs to be adjusted. For example, we noticed that students coming into the advanced classes were often freezing in fencing. They would do one or two things then just stop. So we added additional motions to the first step of every basic drill; at no point in the syllabus any more did the students ever do just one action and stop. Sure enough, the next cohort through didn't have that bad habit.

This process of adjustment will probably go on for years, but it is way easier to adjust a syllabus than create one from scratch. Just remember your goal, and compare the products of the system to the goal it was intended to reach.

If you are planning on researching historical martial arts from historical sources, and creating your own syllabus from scratch, I'd suggest reading my *Theory and Practice of Historical Martial Arts,* which covers everything you need to know to choose a source, interpret it, and develop your syllabus from it.

You can find several examples of syllabi I have created in my books and online:

• *The Medieval Longsword* is a syllabus for learning to use a longsword in the style of Fiore dei Liberi's Art of Arms.

• *The Complete Rapier Workbook* is a syllabus for learning to fence rapier in the style of Capoferro.

• The Syllabus Wiki is a wiki that lays out several of my syllabi in more breadth than you'll find in the books. You can find the wiki here: https://swordschool.com/wiki/index.php/Main_Page

Next up— how do we teach teachers?

PART VII
TRAINING TEACHERS

THE FIVE STAGES OF TEACHER TRAINING

Some people teach because they have an internal need to teach. Others teach because there is an external need from the people around them for a teacher.

People in the first group tend to be a pain in class to start with, because their internal need to learn-by-teaching has them constantly mansplaining the drill to their partner. They need to be shown that they are letting their internal need overwhelm the good of 'their' student, and be given other outlets for their teaching needs.

Those in the second group need a compelling external reason to teach, and it should not be forced upon them.

The key to teaching teachers is the same as for teaching everything else: create an environment in which progression is natural, and failure is not only survivable but expected.

Feedback is essential. As a rule of thumb, always find two things to praise, and one thing that could be worked on. E.g. "Thanks. I can see they're getting it. Especially that tricky step, which you made really clear. Do you think you could get the same effect with less verbal instruction?"

. . .

When teaching people how to teach (as I am trying to do now) what is the goal, the model, and the feedback mechanism?

Many years ago one of my students told me that the best question she had ever been asked about my school was this: "has the instructor improved?" It's a really good indication of the kind of school you are running— does the instructor get better, in such a way that its visible to the students?

The goal is quite simple: you want to be a better teacher, or to understand teaching better, or be able to evaluate the teachers you have access to so you can choose between them. Perhaps it's some combination of these three.

The model is also simple: establish the goal, present a model, and provide feedback mechanisms. I have lots of good models for you to follow, from how to teach a class, or an individual lesson, to creating syllabi that make sense and actually work. Depending on exactly what you are trying to teach, and exactly what your goals are, you can select a model from this book, easily enough.

But creating a feedback mechanism for the teacher is really hard. Ideally, the feedback mechanism needs to be immediate and objective, and clearly indicate success and failure.

What is success? Your student or students improve their skills by learning what you're trying to teach them. You can tell a good teacher by the quality of their students. It's that simple.

But how do you measure that, in real time?

It's quite easy to see whether an individual lesson is working— one expects obvious improvement in the student's skill in minutes. But a class? Here are some possibilities:

1. Student retention. Do they enjoy the class enough to come back?

2. Do they appear to be moving better at the end of the class than at the beginning?

3. Do they remember what they learned from one class to the next?

4. Student evaluations. Ask the students how you are doing, in such a way that they can answer freely and without worrying about your feelings (such as an anonymous suggestions box).

These metrics can give you an idea of whether you are a 'good' teacher or not. But it doesn't necessarily say anything about whether you are *improving* as a teacher. How do we measure that? What is 'success', exactly, and what is 'failure'?

And what is the optimal rate of failure?

One metric where the optimal rate of failure is zero is safety. A good teacher runs a safe class, but you don't work on that by establishing a 40% accident rate. You aim for zero accidents, zero significant injuries. Assuming you're actually training in martial arts, you won't get zero injuries over the course of a decade, but you should aim for it nonetheless.

One where the optimal rate of failure is perhaps 10 or 20% is student dropout rates. If nobody drops out, you're either running a cult, or you have such a low influx of students your club is about to die. It's normal for students to move on in some way— either they find a club they prefer, or move house, or have kids, or change jobs, etc. I would expect to lose some students over the course of a year regardless of how I teach. But if I lose a lot, I have to wonder whether it's my fault.

One possible way to measure success is by tracking cohorts of students through your syllabus. Can you get them to some objective level of proficiency faster this year than you did last? This is made more challenging to measure because every cohort is different, but you should get some idea of whether you're able to generate more learning in less time than you used to be able to.

There is no simple answer to this, and it is probably the very hardest thing to establish in teacher training— so much so, that most teacher training courses don't even try to measure it. But we can do better.

Measure your success as a teacher by the successes of your students, whatever success means to them.

So how do we train teachers? I divide it up into five stages.

Stage 1 practices take place within a normal class under your direction.

'The student' is your teacher-trainee.

Ask the student to take a small group of beginners through the choreography of a basic action, e.g. a footwork drill. This is within a class, so they are not in charge of anything.

Ask the student to teach the choreography of a basic drill to one other person, within a norm.

Ask the student to watch the class as it's running, and tell you what they see. Then ask them what they would teach next. Do we need to take a step back to something simpler, or push them ahead?

Demonstrate with the student in front of the class, often. This gets them used to being onstage.

Adjust the demonstration so that even though you're determining what's happening, they are doing most of the actual demonstration. Give them the fun stuff to show off with.

Stage 2 practices, still within a normal class.

Ask the student to lead the warm-up. Depending on the student, you can either give them time to prepare, or just drop it on them. However it goes, make sure you praise them afterwards, in front of the whole class. "Great job Maaret, that was fun!"

Ask them afterwards how they felt it went, and give them the usual 2 positive responses, one suggestion for improvement.

Ask the student to demonstrate something you have chosen—they call out a demo partner, do the demo as requested. I use any time I'm injured or sick as an excuse to do lots of these first two options. That frames it as "helping out the instructor" not the much more scary "take control of the class". Ask them afterwards how they felt it went, and give them the usual two positive responses, one suggestion for improvement.

When they are comfortable leading the warm-up, ask them what they would follow it with. Whatever they reply, so long as it is at least vaguely on topic, say "good idea. Carry on!" And let them demonstrate it, and have the class practice. This is really where having a familiar class structure is very helpful. They will know what normally comes next, and do something like that. Ask them afterwards how they felt it went, and give them the usual feedback.

Encourage them to be creative in their warm-up leading. If they have some training in something else, let them draw on that. It is not about following exactly what you do, it's about them finding their teaching voice.

Teach them to see the class. Ask the student to watch the class as they're training, and tell you what they see. Then ask them what they would teach next. Do we need to take a step back to something simpler, or push them ahead? Then have them stop the class, demonstrate the new thing, and have the class do it. Ask them afterwards how they felt it went, and give them the usual 2 positive responses, one suggestion for improvement.

Teach them the safety protocols around unsafe training, how to get rid of an unsafe student, how to treat emergencies, basic first aid, etc.

Stage 3 practices

Have the student plan a class from start to finish. Discuss their plan with them. Make it clear that their one true mission for the class is to enable safe training to occur.

Have them run that class, or a part of it, with you there holding the space for them. Feedback as usual from you, but also get their peers to give them feedback, with the usual format: everyone (starting from the lowest in the hierarchy, assuming there is a hierarchy) finds two nice things to say, and makes one suggestion for improvement.

Expect and encourage them to make informed decisions about when to ease back, when to push forward, and to be paying complete attention to the class itself, and the needs of the students in it. "I was going to go on to this more advanced drill, but looking at what they're doing now, I'll have them do this more basic thing first". "They are getting a bit bored, because this is probably a bit too easy for them. I'll mix things up a bit and have them do this thing next". Slavishly following a class plan is death to good teaching.

You might divide the class up into two or more time slots, with one student taking the first section, one the second, etc. Make sure that their plans are compatible though.

Stage 4 practices

When they are comfortable leading a whole class with you there, the next stage is to have them lead all or part of a class, without you there. Make sure they have a peer with them as backup, so they are not alone.

Make time in the schedule for student-lead classes. This is critical: if they don't have the times to practice in, they really can't learn. Accept beforehand that it is better for the long-term good of the Art that students get taught to become teachers, even if that means (as it certainly will) that there will be many classes taught that you could have done better, in that the students present would have maybe improved faster.

When the student is comfortable leading classes with just a peer for support, run an examination. The purpose of the examination is a rite of passage for the candidate: after passing it, they know that they have the authority to run classes on their own account. To be effective, it must be possible to fail, though if the candidate is properly prepared that should never happen. The exam is just a regular class, announced as an exam in advance so the students know what's going on. Here are the four things that will fail a candidate in my Class Leader exams, ranked in order of importance. The candidate is fully aware of all of these, long in advance. No surprises.

1. Allowing unsafe training to occur unchecked. An injury may occur in class even when training is properly conducted, so an injury occurring is not grounds for failing, unless a) the injury was caused by a poorly-supervised environment or b) the candidate fails to handle it. I usually get one or more students to sit out during the exam, and expect the candidate to notice, and find out what's wrong.

2. The candidate talks too much. I use a stopwatch to time everything. If they talk for more than 3 minutes in between exercises, it's a fail. If they have a ratio of more than 1 minute talking for every two minutes training, they fail. So talk/demo for 2 minutes max, have the class practice for 5 minimum. Most candidates have a friend check this for them during their classes leading up to the exam.

3. The candidate can't admit when they are wrong. I will often ask them a question in front of the class, which I know they don't have the answer to. I expect them to answer along the lines of "I don't know, but here's where I would go to find out".

4. Making shit up. We have a syllabus for a reason, and while there is a lot of room to play, the candidate at this level is not there

to teach whatever ideas may pop into their head. The students have a right to expect that any content is within the general bounds of correct practice as we see it in the School. In higher-level exams the student may be presenting their own interpretation of a source, but that expectation must be explicitly set in advance to the students showing up for the class. Mis-remembering a drill is not on its own grounds for failing, but at this level the candidate is supposed to be competent to demonstrate the material in their class plan.

After the exam I go over my notes with the candidate in private, letting them know immediately whether they've passed or failed, and raising any concerns and talking it through, and praising whatever can be praised, before announcing their result to the class. If I have to fail someone, I'll present that to the class as "there were one or two technical issues that we have to polish up, and we'll run another exam for them in a few months". Absolutely never discuss the candidate's failings with the class, but invite them to give the usual 2 for 1 feedback to the candidate if they wish.

Stage 5 practices

Some students want to become professional instructors, or simply keep improving as teachers. There are several further steps that can be taken, such as:

- Training to give an individual lesson. In the individual lesson, the coach controls the fencing environment in real time, adjusting the level of difficulty so that the student improves in the target skill. This is trained for primarily by the general rule in all training, that all drills are practised according to the Rule of Cs. So by the time the student is ready to learn to coach formally, they have already been doing it for years in a less formal way.

- Learning to teach longer classes, such as a full day or full weekend seminar. This is primarily about planning, managing your energy, and applying the class instruction over a longer period.
- Learning to create a training method for a system the student has developed from original research, and to teach that to students. This should also include a feedback mechanism whereby the students' experiences with the material leads to improvements in the interpretation, syllabus construction, and presentation.
- Learning to teach a seminar to an outside group, such as a different club, or at an event such as Swordsquatch, or even one-offs like bachelor party groups. They all have slightly different needs and goals, but the overarching principle is the same: create a safe training space for that group.

PART VIII
EXTRAS

STARTING AND RUNNING A CLUB

One of the most common questions I get asked is this: "there are no HMA clubs near me. What should I do?", and my answer is always the same: "start one". So the next question is "how do I do that?"

The most difficult part of starting a HMA club is deciding to do so. Once the decision has been made, the rest is not so hard.

I've been involved in starting many groups, from the Dawn Duellists' Society in 1994, to the British Federation for Historical Swordplay in 1999, The School of European Swordsmanship in 2001, and literally dozens of satellite clubs since then, so I have some ideas on the subject, as you might imagine.

Let's begin with some general principles.

Starting a group is not as hard as it may seem, it just requires determination, and some basic social skills. The obstacles vary so widely in different countries and cultures that it is very hard to advise on the specifics, but I use a set of basic principles to run my school, which are applicable to any group.

. . .

1. **Group purpose**: every group must have a purpose, clearly stated. "The study and practice of historical swordsmanship" covers most, but you may wish to narrow the focus.

2. **Group needs**: every group has specific needs, which must be met for the group to flourish. Typically they include financial health, sufficient membership, and the specific means to achieve the purpose, such as weapons, treatises and a place to practice.

3. **Individual needs**: every group is comprised of individuals, who will leave if their needs are not met. Such needs include sharing in the common purpose; assistance for beginners, and the various social needs that we all share. Most practitioners prefer a group where they feel welcome and needed, to one where they are looked on with suspicion until they have 'proved' themselves. Even the most inexperienced beginner should be recognised as a vital part of the group: without such beginners, the Art, and the group, have no future.

A GROUP WILL SUCCEED if all the above needs are met, and kept in balance. Once the needs of any one individual (including the illustrious founder) take precedence, the group is doomed. Likewise, any group decision, whether made by the individual in charge, by a committee, or by the whole group, should be arrived at based on how well it serves the three needs. Individuals whose needs are met by the group will stay, and enable the group needs to be met, which enables the group purpose to be met. Of course, many individuals will fall by the wayside when they discover that their needs are not met by a group with that purpose; this is normal, so expect attrition. Also there are some individuals who feel a need to take over any group they join; this is not a problem provided that the group purpose and needs are served by their ascendancy. Just beware of political infighting, and establish the aims of the group clearly enough to prevent slippage.

. . .

Now we have established the principles, let's get into the specifics. You want to start a HMA club: what's the first step?

1. Find a friend who'll have a go at swords. One friend is good; two is better. What, you've got three interested friends? Then this will be easy...

2. Be honest with yourself and your co-founders about your interests, and agree on exactly what, at this stage, the club is going to do. Establish in clear and exact terms the group purpose. For example "we are going to train for HMA tournaments in Longsword and take part in as many as we can". Or "we are going to recreate Meyer's swordsmanship from his book". Or "we are Jedi and will train accordingly". Look for the sources and help you might need. For groups wanting to "recreate Fiore's art of arms", you could use my books, syllabus and so on; but if you want to study Liechtenauer, then those won't be much help. Many of my branches started out as "we will train from this book by this Windsor fellow" and grew from there. Choose, a book, a syllabus, a historical source, even a youtube channel, whatever suits your purpose, and say "we'll do this and only this". It is much better to add things later, once the group is established, than to start out trying to please everyone. To begin with, focus on one thing, and make it absolutely clear what that thing is.

The key question at this stage is 'does being part of this club actually meet my individual needs?' If you wanted a club so you could learn to teach 18th century smallsword, and nobody in this club wants to do smallsword (they're all obsessed with polearms), then start a different club and be clearer about your goals. It is perfectly okay, normal even, for the founders to start the club to scratch their own itch. Start the club you'd want to join.

3. Meet regularly. Once a week minimum, at the same time and in the same place. Depending on the weather and local laws, you

could meet in a park, or (as the DDS did for years) train in a courtyard outside a pub in the centre of Edinburgh. You don't need money for this; there are lots of free spaces, if you just look. When you start out, you will be ignorant and unskilled. That is okay! Everybody starts at zero. But you have SO much more help available than I did in 1992, and I turned out alright. So you will probably do even better.

4. Advertise in any free medium (social media, noticeboards etc.) for like-minded people in your neighbourhood. If you're training in a public space, then be ready for curious people of all ages and types to come up and talk to you. Be very clear about what you are trying to do, so Viking re-enactors won't come along and be disappointed by your sword and buckler club, or vice-versa. Being specific means that people can see in advance whether the club is likely to meet their individual needs.

5. When you have 6-10 people coming regularly, it's time to establish a formal club. Start collecting fees. Price it at the cost of a night out per month, minimum. Eg. in the UK, perhaps £30. In Finland, maybe €40. This is essential. One of the biggest mistakes beginner clubs make is to not gather fees, and they do this mostly because they don't feel they are providing a service that is worth paying for. But you are not selling a service (unless you are setting up a professional school, which I am not covering here), you're gathering the resources the club needs to meet its goals. Members who don't want to pay are not going to help meet the group needs.

What is the money for? To help accomplish the group purpose. You can use it for whatever helps pursue the purpose, such as to pay for a teacher, buy club equipment, send your most active class leaders to events they can't afford to go to on their own, pay for a better venue; the list is endless. My point is that clubs that have money can pursue their purpose much more easily than those that don't. I advise having members use a 'set it and forget it' direct debit or paypal regular payment; it's much more effective than manually collecting dues.

6. At this stage you will need to register a non-profit organisation. This is usually quite easy to do, if you don't mind filling in forms. Use whatever umbrella organisations are available. University students can start a University society to get access to University facilities. Your local sports fencing club might let you set up a sub-group within their umbrella (as, for instance, my branch in Oulu, Finland, did). If there is a suitable umbrella available, consider joining it. Be careful that doing so does not interfere with your group purpose, though. If joining an umbrella organisation means giving up your core purpose, or unacceptable changes to equipment or rules, then don't do it.

Be careful that you understand the rules around what a non-profit organisation can and cannot do. I can't advise you on the law in your country, but in general, you can hire a teacher (but the employee cannot usually be part of the governing board). You cannot use the funds to pay for your personal sword collection. You will also probably have to file annual accounts and a list of members. This is not too much work if there are many hands helping; maybe one person handles the paperwork; another handles finding new members; a few others run regular classes. At this stage the thing to watch out for is that the individual needs of the people doing all the work are being met. Some kind of compensation for their efforts is appropriate (such as not having to pay dues, or subsidised attendance at an event, or a guarantee of never having to clean the training space, or something). The last thing you want is for the essential administration to not get done because the overworked volunteer doing it has been snowed under mounds of paper and can't get to class, so quits. Look after your officers, they deserve it.

And there you have it. It's really not so complicated. It is a lot of work though, but that's true of almost everything worthwhile.

TEACHING FROM A SHOPPING LIST

One of the issues that I face as an itinerant swordsmanship instructor, presiding over a school that exists on three continents, is that I can only visit each branch occasionally. I encourage the branches to ask for what they want, to be actively engaged with their own training. I also encourage all students in regular class to ask for the material they are most interested in, or feel they need to cover next. This means that the group I am teaching on any given day will tend to have a list of material that they would like me to cover, which is often pretty haphazard. For example, before one seminar I received this email:

> Here are some wishes for the seminar from the intermediates and class leaders:
>
> 1) How to train with someone who is much stronger than you? How to prove that their technique is wrong if they succeed in it only because of their strength?
>
> 2) How to get the most out of training with a beginner? How to benefit from this situation?

3) Safe ways of training and ergonomics at work. Maybe focus on shoulders?

4) 2nd drill stretto (there were some confusion about the way it should be done correctly).

5) Punta falsa.

6) Could we learn some Vadi techniques?

PS. There will be beginners attending to this seminar. They know some techniques with dagger, but haven't probably learned all parts of the 1st and 2nd drills yet.

As you can see, there is not much obvious connection between teaching the stretto form of second drill, and teaching students to train with others that are much stronger or much less experienced than they are. I spotted a teaching opportunity, and so began the seminar by discussing this list with the students present, and explaining to them the order in which we were going to do everything, and why.

The first step was to identify the most general item. In this case ergonomics, because correct form and structure are required for everything you ever do, in the salle and out. So we spent quite a long time working on perfect push-ups, perfect squats, and the structural foundation of Fiore's movement dynamics.

Then, using ergonomics as our base, we moved on to the skill of how to use a beginner partner to develop your own skills. This is a very common request, and given that since I came to Finland in 2001 the vast majority of the people I have crossed swords with have been my students, I have an awful lot of experience in making less experienced training partners nonetheless useful. There are basically three ways to do it: you either take advantage of their unpredictability to create genuinely random drills to train your responsiveness; or within the bounds of a set drill, you demonstrate perfect form, because they will copy your every mistake; or in a competitive drill, you aim to win by the narrowest possible margin. We used the standing step drill as a good example of this last idea, and I demonstrated with someone clearly smaller and weaker than myself, who had been training for about a month. By allowing her to push me to the very limit of my balance I was able to use the minimal resistance she was able to give to practice at the edge of my skill.

This introduced the idea of customising your actions to the specific training partner that you have, and in this case how, without being dramatically more skilful, you can train a beginner out of using their superior strength. There is nothing wrong with strength: strength is good, skill is better, strength applied skilfully is best of all. The trick of course, is to make it so that if they stiffen up, their action fails; but if they execute the action in a relaxed way it succeeds. They will only learn to let go of their strength if they don't need it. We used the third and fourth plays of the first master of the dagger as our example plays for this exercise. I then had them all look for actions which made themselves tense up, to understand better the problem of relying on strength, and within the context of those actions, focus on using only the minimum necessary force.

So, with ergonomics underpinning all, and focussed experience in working usefully with the beginner, and working usefully with a much stronger partner, we can then address the system-specific technical requests.

We started with the cutting drill, emphasising shoulder stabilisation from the perfect push-ups, and I spotted and corrected some branch-wide errors. We then used a sword handling drill to focus on correct ergonomics for holding the sword. From there we went into first drill, and use that as the basis for working on the *punta falsa*. At this stage, those that had difficulty with the basic drill were separated out and worked on that. We needed to make sure that the mechanics of the *punta falsa* were clearly understood, which our ergonomics study had prepared us for. Then the two groups were put back together, with the seniors required to make sure that when they attacked, as the blades met the circumstances were correct for the defender's set response; and when they defended, they had to respond correctly to the exact conditions of the blade relationship that actually occurred. This made them work on parts 1 and 2 of the 'training with beginners' theory above.

From there we went into second drill, and built the stretto form of it step-by-step from the basic, largo, form. Again, those that didn't know the basic form were taught that, and those that did learned the more difficult stretto version. This was classic, straightforward teaching basic drills from the syllabus. The trick was to connect them explicitly to the foundational skills we worked on before, namely ergonomics, using beginners, and dealing with stronger partners. Of course the stretto forms of the drills explicitly deal with resistant partners, so fit nicely with the theme.

By finishing up with the stretto form of second drill, we had introduced the zogho stretto situation, and so it was easy to segue into spending the last hour working on Vadi's solutions to the zogho stretto, and why they differ from Fiore's.

To summarise, the process of teaching from a list of requests goes:

1. Identify the most generally applicable concept, start with that

2. Take each request in order of specificity, from most generally applicable, to the most specific

3. Organise the parts into a logical sequence, paying particular attention to the connections between the items on your list

4. Make the organisation of the material part of the lesson, so that the students can see how their requests are being dealt with.

KEY CONCEPTS REVIEW

Do you understand everything on this list? Make your own notes to clarify your thinking around each idea. These are deliberately in no particular order. Can you think why that might be?

- Use only positive statements.
- Every drill, technique or action should be a solution to a problem that the student has experienced.
- Every drill should be trained at the optimal rate of failure, which is usually 20-40%. So the action should work about 60-80% of the time.
- Use your multipliers to create sufficient complexity to generate the optimal rate of failure.
- Your multipliers are: the Rule of Cs (choreography-coaching-competition), add a step, degrees of freedom, who moves first.
- All training follows this pattern: Run a diagnostic, fix the weakest link, run the diagnostic again.

- Choreography is a useful beginning but a useless ending. We are not dancers.
- Talk less, do more.
- It's not about you. It's about them.
- No injuries.
- The Pareto Principle: 20% of causes produce 80% of outcomes. What 20% should your students be focussed on?
- Breadth is important because it enables us to make an informed choice about what to go deep on: but depth beats breadth every time.
- Distinguish between knowledge and skill. We teach knowledge, and coach skill.
- Distinguish between technical and tactical. A technical problem is doing the right thing, but not well enough. A tactical problem is doing the wrong thing.
- Mindful practice is the key to creating depth. But a bit of friendly bish bash bosh is good too.
- Structure and flow: if your class is not flowing, change its structure. To improve your students' structure, make them flow into it.
- At any given time, teach just ONE THING.

ABOUT THE AUTHOR

Consulting Swordsman Dr. Guy Windsor is acclaimed and respected both as a teacher and a pioneering researcher of medieval and renaissance martial arts. He began his professional historical martial arts career when he founded The School of European Swordsmanship in Helsinki, Finland in 2001. Awarded a PhD by Edinburgh University for his seminal work recreating historical combat systems, Guy has written numerous training manuals and workbooks for historical martial artists, and he has travelled the world as an in-demand teacher and lecturer, and even developed the card game Audatia – bringing the thrills of historic swordfighting to the modern gaming audience. He has also created a huge range of online courses, covering medieval knightly combat, sword and buckler, rapier, remedial training, and even how to train alone. Now, Guy splits his time between researching historical martial arts; writing books and creating online courses, teaching students all over the world; and working as a consulting expert. He runs the popular historical martial arts podcast The Sword Guy, interviewing historical martial artists and experts from a wide range of related disciplines.

You can find him and his work online at swordschool.com.

MORE BOOKS BY GUY

If you've enjoyed this book you should definitely visit swordschool.com and sign up for my newsletter. There's never any spam, and you'll get the news first about new releases and giveaways.

Looking for a community of sword people? Then come and join my social media space SwordPeople.Com No ads, no algorithms, no bots, no trolls. Just nice people talking swords.

You may also like the following:

Training manuals and workbooks:

The Duellist's Companion: the classic guide to the rapier fencing of Ridolfo Capoferro

This was originally published in 2006, and I updated it and published the second edition in 2023.

The Rapier Workbooks: workbooks comprise a complete training method for becoming proficient at Capoferro's style of rapier fencing. Each workbook is designed to lie flat, with abundant space for note-taking, and with a linked video clip for every action. They are available laid out for right or left handers, to make note-taking easier.

The Rapier Workbook Part 1, Beginners (you can get the ebook version free at guywindsor.net/tdcextras)

The Rapier Workbook Part 2, Completing the Basics

The Rapier Workbook Part 3, Developing Your Skills

The Rapier Workbook Part 4, Sword and Dagger and Sword and Cape.

I have also compiled the four workbooks into one volume, *The Complete Rapier Workbook.*

The Armizare Workbook, part one: Beginners Course. This workbook includes detailed instruction, videos, and (in the printed versions) space for notes. It also allows the student to choose their own path through the material, with options presented at every stage.

Mastering the Art of Arms, Book 1: The Medieval Dagger. A training manual for Fiore's dagger techniques. This is a complete overview of the dagger material in Fiore's art of arms, and includes instruction on how to fall, how to develop real skills, as well as covering all of the fundamental attacks with and defences against the dagger. Hardback available from Spada Press, paperback and ebook from Freelance Academy Press.

Mastering the Art of Arms, Book 2: The Medieval Longsword. A training manual for Fiore's longsword plays. If you want to learn how to train and fight with a longsword in an authentic medieval style, this book is for you. This book features an introduction by the excellent historical novelist and medieval combatant, Christian Cameron.

Mastering the Art of Arms, Book 3: Advanced Longsword, Form and Function. This covers using forms for skill development, and a lot of Fiore-specific training, building on the groundwork laid in The Medieval Longsword.

The Swordsman's Companion. A training manual for medieval

longsword. This was my first book, published in 2004, and it has become something of a classic in this field. As a training manual, it is largely replaced by *The Medieval Longsword*, but as a book about how and why to train, it is still relevant.

Academic, Overview, and Other works:

From Medieval Manuscript to Modern Practice: the Longsword Techniques of Fiore dei Liberi. This has my transcription, translation, commentary, and links to video clips of my interpretation of all of Fiore's longsword plays on foot out of armour, as well as a thorough introduction.

From Medieval Manuscript to Modern Practice: the Wrestling Techniques of Fiore dei Liberi. This has my transcription, translation, commentary, and links to video clips of my interpretation of all of Fiore's *abrazare*, or wrestling, plays as well as a thorough introduction.

The Principles and Practices of Solo Training. The self-help book for people who want to add years to their life and life to their years. In this refreshingly straightforward and gentle guide I lay out the fundamental principles behind personal development and excellence in any field. How? By establishing a solid foundation, and a step-by-step approach to mechanics and training.

The Theory and Practice of Historical Martial Arts. This book includes all seven instalments of The Swordsman's Quick Guide, as well as extensive instruction on recreating historical martial arts from historical sources, how to train, how to teach, even how to get better sleep.

Swordfighting, for Writers, Game Designers, and Martial Artists. This book is made up of about 50% posts from my blog and 50% new material, and does exactly what it says in the title. It also features an introduction from the one and only Neal Stephenson, author of *Snow Crash, The Diamond Age, The Mongoliad,* and *The Baroque Cycle,* to name but a few.

The Art of Sword Fighting in Earnest. An accurate translation of Filippo Vadi's *De Arte Gladiatoria Dimicandi*, with a detailed introduction, commentary from a practical swordsmanship perspective, and a full glossary. This book was examined as part of my PhD, so it's been academically vetted at the highest level.

If you prefer to learn from audio or video, check out my online courses at https://courses.swordschool.com.

And remember to go to guywindsor.net/writingtmresources where you'll find your free templates, and links to other useful resources. Sign up for the mailing list while you're there, of course!

ACKNOWLEDGEMENTS

Thanks are due first to my wife Michaela, who is unfailingly tolerant of the bizarre lifestyle that being a historical martial arts instructor and author seems to require. My assistant Katie Mackenzie is extraordinarily good at all the admin and spreadsheets and check-box checking that goes into actually publishing and marketing my work. I doubt you'd be holding this book without her help. Mark Teppo did an excellent job on the editing— I ceded the point on that Oxford comma by way of thanks!

As regards learning how to teach, I've been influenced by my own teachers, primarily: Steve Fox, Sujit Wings, Prof. Philip Bruce. And students who materially contributed to my own teaching skill, mostly by telling me when things weren't working: Topi Mikkola, Tomi Förstí, Auri Poso, Jaana Wessman, Greg Galistan, Chris Blakey, Petri Piira, Maaret Sirkkala. Colleagues and friends who have provided teaching advice, inspiration, and feedback include: Auri Poso, Joeli Takala, David Biggs, Sean Hayes, Leonard Voelker, Jessica Finley, Ilpo Jalamo, Kaj Westersund, Luis Preto, Thomas Stoeppler, Andrew Somlyo.

Perhaps the deepest instruction on how physical skills are learned has come from watching my children growing and learning over the last 17 years. So thanks also to Grace and Katrina, for that and everything else. It's been a holy terror, joy beyond measure, and a privilege beyond imagining.

Milton Keynes UK
Ingram Content Group UK Ltd.
UKHW050215021124
450461UK00003B/11

9 789527 157084